S0-BCO-002

Collector's Guide to
BOOKENDS

Identification and Values

Louis Kuritzky

COLLECTOR BOOKS
A Division of Schroeder Publishing Co., Inc.

The current values in this book should be used only as a guide. They are not intended to set prices, which vary from one section of the country to another. Auction prices as well as dealer prices vary greatly and are affected by condition as well as demand. Neither the Authors nor the Publisher assumes responsibility for any losses that might be incurred as a result of consulting this guide.

Searching For A Publisher?

We are always looking for knowledgeable people considered to be experts within their fields. If you feel that there is a real need for a book on your collectible subject and have a large comprehensive collection, contact Collector Books.

Front cover: Top: Queen of the Nile, Ronson, 1924; Center: Keyhole View, 1926; Bottom left: Seated Man Reading, J.B. Hirsch; Bottom right: Lighting the Way, J.B. Hirsch.

Cover design by Terri Stalions
Book design by Mary Ann Dorris

Dedication

Loving thanks to my wife, Virginia, and children Arielle and Zeth, each of whom made personal contributions to completing this volume in a variety of memorable ways.

Additional copies of this book may be ordered from:

COLLECTOR BOOKS
P.O. Box 3009
Paducah, Kentucky 42002-3009

@$19.95. Add $2.00 for postage and handling.

Copyright © 1998 by Louis Kuritzky

This book or any part thereof may not be reproduced
without the written consent of the Author and Publisher.

CONTENTS

 INTRODUCTION

I bought my very first pair of bookends (Sajous Cyclopedia), in Pittsburgh, Pennsylvania, in the company of my dearly beloved mother-in-law, Marjorie Sloan. At the time, I knew nothing of antiques, and less about bookends. I needed a pair of bookends because my personal book collection had overrun the bookcases, and I was now resorting to stacking them on top, with the intended help of bookends.

I had hoped for some really heavy iron thing, since I remembered my own mother possessing such pieces, but was surprised at the prices these old pieces commanded. Desiring some reference information on bookends, I was told (repeatedly), that this did not exist. After seeing a number of quite charming pairs of bookends, I set out to provide information to the obviously bookend-information-starved populace.

The first book ever published on bookends appeared in 1996 (Seecof, Seecof & Kuritzky, *Bookend Revue,* published by Schiffer). Since then, a bookend collector club was begun with a quarterly newsletter; this book that you possess has been added, *Cast Metal Bookends* (General McBride, Schiffer Publishers, 1997) has been published, and added to the informative *Figurative Cast Iron* (Douglas Congdon-Martin, Schiffer, 1994), giving the bookend enthusiast a wealth of information.

This book is weighted specifically towards metal bookends. Most bookend collectors pay primary attention to metal, with peripheral interest to ceramics, pottery, glass, or synthetic materials (e.g., Lucite, Bakelite). As more people become interested in the field, the knowledge progressively expands. This volume contains items never previously published, in particular a wide selection of Gorham bronze bookends, highly sought after by serious collectors. Many people contributed to this publication, and my thanks to those of you willing to share your collections, and those dealers who generously allowed photos taken of their pieces. Special thanks to David Surgan of New York for his contributions on Heintz Art Metal Works; Richard Weinstein of Long Island, New York, for his contributions on Ronson; Sue Benoliel for her eclectic collection of pieces shared; Jay Mendlovitz of San Antonio, Texas, for sharing his collection; and Michael Horseman for his insights on and collection of depression glass animals.

PREFACE

COLLECTING

Until recently, bookends have hardly been considered a collectible in their own right. Rather, if you were a penguin collector, you might pick up some penguin bookends; if you were a militaria person, you'd get some military bookends. General antiques enthusiasts have recognized the inherent beauty and symmetry of pairs of bookends. A wide diversity of art styles abound in bookend art, so whether you are the arts and crafts type, the Art Deco type, or the kitsch type, there is plenty to look for. Additionally, bookends remain within the economic reach of persons of even modest means, so one can build a delightful collection without extravagance. Of personal appeal to me, and some others, is the usefulness of bookends. I am not one to obtain something and lock it in a vault for protection. Many bookends are as pristine as they are because they have been sheltered during years of quiet support on the bookshelves of our predecessors. This is not to say that one could not fashion a collection of aristocratic pieces; for instance, you will note there are examples of bookends with price tags in the $3,000 – $7,500 range, but these pieces are extraordinary, and typically only seen once or twice in huge shows of 1,000 or more dealers.

CONFIGURATIONS

Most bookends are easily distinguished as such, but some pieces are dubiously designated. For instance, old cast iron sadirons (flatirons) are often used for bookends, as are heavy miniature watering pails, flower pots, and an endless variety of other pieces, yet, they are not really bookends. Although there are a few exceptions, bookends will have a definite vertical plane of contact with the books. Some contact points are fragile or small in area. For instance, "Appeal to the Great Spirit", (p. 76) is generally accepted as bookends, yet the outstretched arm of the Indian is the readily noted contact point. Unfortunately, since this piece is made of relatively soft cast gray metal, it is easily bent or broken, and numerous examples of this piece have been seen with damaged arms.

There is much discussion on what is the "right" configuration for pairs of bookends: should figures be facing in opposite directions, like a right and left glove? Are pieces that are identical really a pair, or should they be reflections. Apparently, there are numerous correct configurations, as reputable art metal crafters have produced a variety of them. There are a few circumstances where the two bookends are intentionally different from one another, as in Plate 186, (p. 52), where the sculptures are complementary, but distinctly different.

You will often see orphan bookends that have been transformed into doorstops. The size and weightiness of doorstops usually make them easily separated from bookends, but on occasion the distinction may not be absolute.

Buying single bookends is not a bad idea. You should generally anticipate paying for a single about one third or less of the price of a pair. Some pieces have unusually vulnerable aspects: extended arms or legs that protrude from the figure; celluloid faces or hands glued into place; or another thin projection susceptible to trauma. If you see a single bookend, keep in mind before purchase:

1) A rare piece will be even more rare to discover twice as a single. Unless you believe the piece is level 4 or less in rarity, your likelihood of finding a well-matched partner for it is very small.

2) Common pieces are just that, and you <u>are</u> likely to find a mate.

3) Pieces that have vulnerable parts most often show up as singles — their partners have been damaged and discarded.

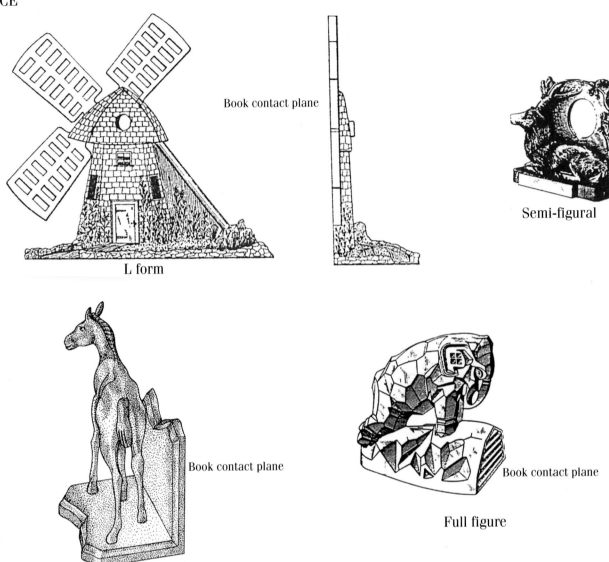

Book contact plane

L form

Semi-figural

Book contact plane

L form with full figure

Book contact plane

Full figure

ABOUT THIS BOOK

In this text, captions describe the name, date, maker, material, size, markings, rarity, and value of pieces. If names are designated on the piece, or the piece represents an artwork of known name, that name given. If the manufacturer names the piece in their catalog, that name is generally used (which is why, for instance, certain Ronson pieces in this volume differ from *Bookend Revue*; company names were discovered in Ronson catalogs and replaced the previously designated names). Dates were ascertained from catalogs, markings, and similarities to other pieces. When known, the date is simply printed; if the date is being estimated, it is listed as "ca. 19XX".

When the maker is known, it is listed. Several companies are known only by their initials, and are so listed. Other pieces are clearly made by the same company, but that company name is unknown. Since it is known they are all from the same source, unknown companies with obvious multiple pieces have been designated X-1, X-2, X-3, etc., so that you can at least know that the same company produced a particular piece, even though we lack certainty who the company is. Pieces which appear likely to be produced by a particular company are printed as attr. XXX, meaning attributed to XXX. Material was assessed by direct examination, but since metals are not precisely identifiable without sophisticated scientific techniques, undoubtedly there are some which eluded specific identification. Size is given in inches and refers to greatest height.

RARITY AND VALUE

Rarity value was assessed on a 5-point scale. Pieces seen only once are designated **5***.
1: **Unusually common**: found consistently in almost every flea market or mall; always available.
2: **Very common**: found routinely in malls and flea markets; consistently available.
3: **Common**: found mostly in antique stores, occasionally in flea markets; frequently available when sought for.
4: **Uncommon**: not routinely found even in antique shops; likely to require a substantial investment of both time searching and money expended to obtain.
5: **Rare**: seen occasionally even by experienced antiquers; infrequently available, even at large shows.

The rarity of pieces has been determined by my personal perusal of many thousands of antique dealers. My occupation as an itinerant educator has allowed me opportunity to spend at least two days each week someplace different, all across the United States. Certainly, there are some regional differences, e.g., Art Deco and Art Nouveau are both more prevalent and more expensive on the coasts, especially in large cities (Los Angeles, New York, San Francisco). Nonetheless, there is a certain consistency in availability observed over the long run. Depending on your geography, some of my analysis may belie your personal experience. For instance, the New Bedford Whaler I have seen four times in six years, but always in the New England states. So, a New Englander might say the piece merits a **4** rarity, but Midwesterners might think it merits a **5***. I have done my best to accommodate these variations.

Price has been established based upon similar experience. Since I also have sold bookends at antique shows and malls within the range of prices quoted here, I do not think the prices unreasonable. No doubt you will find great variation in price, as I have seen prices vary tenfold for the same piece at a single antique show! Price is shown for the piece in very good condition. Pieces in outstanding condition merit substantially greater price, and the reverse is the case, of course, for less well maintained pieces. Generally, a single piece will sell for a third or less the price of a pair. You may anticipate dealers will buy pieces they feel likely to sell at a third to a half their probable retail price.

Note that rarity and price are not always linked. For instance, some promotional pieces, perhaps issued by a company as an employee reward, are decidedly rare, but not very valuable. As in all other markets, the price is a distillation of the forces of supply and demand.

Because the field of bookend collecting is still quite new, there is huge opportunity to obtain very desirable pieces at quite reasonable prices. Reproductions do not yet cause a major stir in the bookend world, with the exception of Roseville, which is usually not an area of primary interest to bookend collectors.

Glass, ceramic, and pottery bookends are less represented than metal. This reflects the fact that most bookend collectors are primarily interested in metal, and that the more noteworthy pieces (Rookwood, Roseville, Fulper, Cowan, Frankoma) are already well catalogued in texts specifically dealing with these companies.

Readers are invited to submit inquiry, information, correction, or items of interest to the author.

FEMALE FIGURES

Plate 1. Kneeling Nude, ca. 1933, gray metal, 5", rarity 4, $140.00.

Plate 2. Nude Kneeling on Pedestal, ca. 1933, Bronzart, gray metal, 7", rarity 4, $175.00.

Plate 3. Hands Down, ca. 1925, iron, 5¾", #323, rarity 5*, $135.00.

Plate 4. Seated and Standing Ladies, ca. 1925, iron, 5" and 8", THEW, rarity 5, $250.00.

Plate 5. Not Quite Bookish, ca. 1930, K&O, gray metal, 8", shopmark, rarity 5, $225.00.

Plate 6. Nude on Book, ca. 1929, Littco, iron, 8", shopmark (not always marked), rarity 4, $160.00.

Plate 7. Lorenzl Lady, Petite, ca. 1930, Ronson, gray metal, 5¾", company tag #16532, rarity 5, $210.00.

Plate 8. Lorenzl Lady (Ronson), ca. 1924, Ronson, gray metal, 9", company tag #12307, rarity 5, $425.00.

Plate 10. Wisdom Well, ca. 1929, iron, 5½", rarity 4, $95.00.

Plate 9. Lorenzl Lady, ca. 1922, Austria, bronze, Lorenzl, Austria, 9", rarity 5*, $3,500.00.

Plate 11. Mournful Lady, ca. 1928, Littco, iron, 6", rarity 5, $195.00. Also seen in bronze patina.

Plate 12. Well of Wisdom, ca. 1929, Connecticut Foundry, iron, 6", shopmark, Well of Wisdom, 1929, rarity 5, $175.00.

Plate 13. Girl in the Circle, ca. 1925, X-2, iron, 5¼", #17, rarity 5*, $195.00.

Plate 14. Nude with Sash (multi-tier pedestal), ca. 1929, X - 2, iron, 5½", rarity 5, $250.00.

Plate 15. Nude with Sash (single-tier pedestal), ca. 1929, X - 2, iron, 5", rarity 4, $175.00.

Plate 16. Girl in Wreath, ca. 1929, X-2, iron, 6¼", rarity 5, $195.00.

Plate 17. Scarf Dance, ca. 1920, attr. X-2, iron, 6½", #15, rarity 5, $195.00

Plate 18. Dancing Ladies with Drape, ca. 1928, bronze, 6½", rarity 5, $225.00.

Plate 19. Nude with Drape, ca. 1928, Verona, iron, shopmark, 6¾", rarity 4, $135.00.

Plate 20. Draped Nymph, 1920, Ronson, gray metal on marbelized metal base, 8", LV Aronson, 1920, company tag #12303M, rarity 5, $350.00.

Plate 21. Lady in Red, ca. 1932, Crescent Metal Works, gray metal, 9", company tag, rarity 5*, $275.00.

Plate 21A. Shopmark, Crescent Metal Works, with company tag.

Plate 22. Nouveau Dance, ca. 1920, iron, approx. 5⅛", #306, rarity 5*, $175.00.

Plate 23. As With Wings, ca. 1925, iron, 9", rarity 5, $275.00.

Plate 24. In the Clouds, ca. 1925, X-2, 6", iron, #73, rarity 5, $150.00.

Plate 25. Curtseying Lady, ca. 1925, X-2, iron, 7½", #52, rarity 5, $195.00. Also seen in antiqued red finish.

Plate 26. Tapestry Dancer, ca. 1925, iron, 7¼", rarity 5, $175.00.

Plate 27. Loie, 1927 (pictured in 1927 Sears catalog), X-1, gray metal, 7", #500, rarity 4, $265.00. (An identical piece is manufactured by Art Metal Works, marked AMW, rarity 5*, $295.00.) Multiple finishes seen: beige, bronze, polychrome, black brown, depression green.

Plate 28. March Girl, ca. 1925, Acorn Company, bronze, 7", shopmark, March Girl, No.601, rarity 5, $225.00.

Plate 29. Keyhole View, 1926, iron, 7½", rarity 4, $165.00. (This piece is design patent #69,502 to designer Jeanne Druicklieb, NY, NY, February 23, 1926.)

Plate 30. Eve, ca. 1925, iron, 6¾", rarity 4, $110.00.

Plate 31. Miss Moderne, ca. 1929, iron, 6½", Miss Moderne, rarity 4, $115.00.

Plate 32. Nude on Pedestal, ca. 1933, gray metal, 8", rarity 4, $165.00.

Plate 33. Hanging the Moon, ca. 1930, gray metal with marble, 5½", rarity 5*, $225.00.

Plate 34. Modest Maiden, ca. 1930, gray metal, 7", #520, rarity 5, $325.00.

Andromeda

The story of Andromeda in Greek mythology relates that she was an Ethiopian princess, daughter of King Cepheus and Queen Cassiopeia. Poseidon, god of the sea and father of the sea-goddesses called Nereids, was angered when Cassiopeia bragged that Andromeda's beauty surpassed that of the Nereids. He sent a sea monster to assail Ethiopia, and was only to be mollified by the sacrifice of Andromeda herself. The hero Perseus found Andromeda chained to a sea cliff, rescued her, and killed the monster. The monster was turned into the first sea coral by Poseidon. Perseus married Andromeda; they later became king and queen of Tiryns.

Plate 35. Andromeda, ca. 1910, gray metal, 6½", signed Alliot, emblem: "Andromede, par A. Alliot", rarity 5*, $275.00.

Plate 36. Sleeping Beauty, ca. 1925, Niobe, iron, 6¼", rarity 5, $250.00.

Plate 37. Seated Pose, ca. 1930, gray metal, 6¾", Made in USA, rarity 5, $325.00. (Compare with Plate 128, Modest Maiden; although similar, there are significant differences.)

Plate 38. Asian Maiden on the Wall, ca. 1925, iron, 5", rarity 5*, $110.00.

Plate 39. Art Deco Nude, ca. 1932, JB Hirsch, 8¾", gray metal, 8¾", #518, rarity 5, $250.00.

Plate 40. Nymph on Dolphin, gray metal, ca. 1929.5¾", rarity 5*, $175.00.

Plate 41. Girl Posing, ca. 1947, Dodge, gray metal, company tag, 7", rarity 5, $170.00.

Plate 41A. Shopmark, Dodge, Inc.

Plate 42. Butterfly Girl, ca. 1927, X-1, gray metal, 7", #63, rarity 5, $375.00 (polychrome), $325.00 (other finishes).

Plate 43. Modesty, ca. 1920, Ronson, gray metal, 5¾", company tag #12301, rarity 5*, $325.00.

Plate 44. Outrageous, ca. 1930, Gotham Art Bronze, bronze clad, 6½", company label, rarity 5, $250.00. (Collection of Sue Benoliel)

Plate 45. Arching Lady, ca. 1929, iron, 4¾", rarity 5, $175.00. (This design has been produced in a variety of materials; the most common is gray metal, rarity 4, $150.00.)

Plate 46. Vine Entwined Lady, ca. 1928, Armor Bronze, bronze clad, artist signature, date, 5", rarity 5*, $250.00. (Collection of Sue Benoliel)

Plate 47. Tambourine Girl, 1926, Gift House, Inc., iron, 5¼", Gift House, Inc. 1926, rarity 4, $110.00.

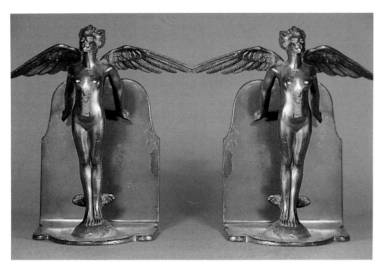

Plate 48. Winged Nymph, ca. 1925, Ronson, gray metal, 5", company tag #11782, rarity 5, $300.00.

Plate 49. Dance Pose, ca. 1932, K&O, gray metal, 6¾", shopmark, rarity 5, $150.00.

Plate 50. Butterfly Dancer, ca. 1925, bronze, 7½", rarity 5*, $325.00. (This piece is also produced in gray metal with gold finish by K&O, rarity 5, $350.00.)

Plate 51. Dancing Girl, ca. 1924, Ronson, gray metal, 5", company tag #11781, rarity 5*, $295.00.

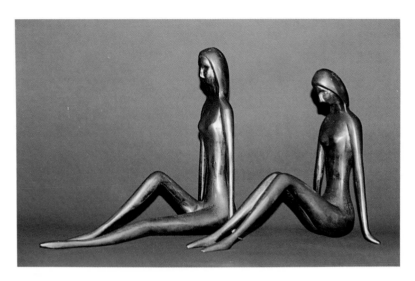

Plate 52. Nude with Mirror, ca. 1922, attr. Pompeian Bronze, bronze clad, 6½", rarity 5, $175.00.

Plate 53. Back to Back Girls, ca. 1940, brass, 7¾", rarity 5*, $175.00.

Plate 55. Tango Deco, 1930, C Company, iron, 6", C Co., 1930 rarity 5*, $225.00.

Plate 54. Nude with Dogs, ca. 1929, iron, 7", copyright symbol, #269, rarity 5, $195.00.

Plate 56. Aztec Archer, ca. 1925, iron, 7½", rarity 5*, $150.00.

Plate 57. Lost Hope, ca. 1930, K&O, gray metal, shopmark, rarity 4, $125.00 (polychrome), $95.00 (other finishes).

Plate 58A. Shopmark, Jennings Brothers.

Plate 58. Lady of the Theater, ca. 1924, Jennings Brothers, gray metal, 5", shopmark, #1529, rarity 5, $250.00. Also in beige finish.

Plate 59. Tip Toes, ca. 1925, Pompeian Bronze, bronze clad, 10", shopmark, rarity 5, $325.00.

Plate 60. Thespian, ca. 1925, iron, 5½", #140, rarity 4, $115.00.

Plate 61. Anchor Lady, ca. 1928, gray metal with celluloid head and hands, on marble base, 8½", rarity 5, $300.00.

Plate 62. Girl on Bench, ca. 1925, gray metal with celluloid face and hands, on marble base, 6⅛", rarity 5, $350.00.

Plate 63. Queen of the Nile, 1924 Ronson, gray metal, 6", rarity 5, $375.00 (polychrome), $350.00 (other finishes).

Plate 63A. Polychrome of Plate 63.

Plate 64. Nefruari, ca. 1928, gray metal with celluloid face and hands, on marble base, 9", rarity 5*, $325.00.

Plate 65. Pixie Girl, ca. 1927, attr. JB Hirsch, gray metal on marble base, 5¼", rarity 5, $275.00.

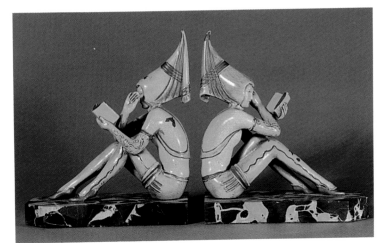

Plate 66. Gerdago Girl, ca. 1927, JB Hirsch, gray metal with celluloid face, on marble base, 7¼", rarity 5*, $550.00.

Plate 67. Deco Warm Up, ca. 1925, gray metal and celluloid, on marble base, rarity 5*, $600.00. (Courtesy Shand Antiques, Toronto, Canada)

Plate 68. Dreaming, ca. 1930, gray metal, approx. 7", rarity 5*, $150.00.

FEMALE FIGURES

Plate 69. Platinum Girls, ca. 1927, attr. Greist, Inc., gray metal, 7", rarity 5, $250.00.

Plate 70. Deco Bust, 1947, Abbot, gray metal, 7¼", Abbot Schy 47, rarity 5, $150.00.

Plate 71. Maiden, ca. 1930, Frankart, gray metal, 6", shop-mark, rarity 5, $225.00.

Plate 72. Duclos Deco, ca. 1930, Duclos, gray metal, 7½", Duclos, rarity 5*, $275.00.

Plate 73. Portrait of a Lady, ca. 1930, Ronson, gray metal, company tag #16176, 6½" rarity 5, $300.00. Collection of Richard Weistein.

Plate 74. Demure, ca. 1928, gray metal, approx. 4½", rarity 5, $175.00.

Plate 75. Lady Face, ca. 1940, New Martinsville, 5¼", rarity 5, $200.00.

Plate 76. Cameo Girls, 1926, iron, 4¼", rarity 4, $75.00.

Plate 77. Spinning Scene, ca. 1930, iron, 4⅞", rarity 3, $50.00.

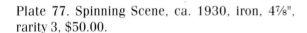

Plate 78. Minerva, ca. 1925, attr. Judd, iron, 5¾", #9726, rarity 5, $110.00 (as an expandable, rarity 4, $85.00).

FEMALE FIGURES

Plate 79. Knowledge, 1925, Pompeian Bronze, gray metal, 4¼", Knowledge, PB, 1925, rarity 4, $175.00.

Plate 80. Meditation (PB), 1925, Pompeian Bronze, gray metal, 5¼", Pompeian Bronze, Meditation, 1925, rarity 4, $175.00.

Plate 81. Shepherdess, ca. 1925, Pompeian Bronze Co., gray metal, 5", rarity 4, $135.00.

Plate 82. Aurora, ca. 1925, bronze, 4¾", rarity 5*, $225.00.

Plate 83. Your Book, Sir, 1924, Ronson, gray metal, LV Aronson, 1924, 5½", rarity 5*, $175.00.

Plate 84. Madrigale, 1925, Pompeian Bronze, gray metal, 4½", Madrigale, PB, Inc, 1925, rarity 4, $75.00.

Plate 85. Maiden's Fountain, ca. 1928, solid bronze, bronze, approx. 5", rarity 4, $175.00.

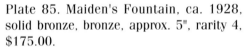

Plate 86. Girl at Fountain, ca. 1923, X-1, gray metal, 5", #503, rarity 5, $275.00.

Plate 87. Jeanne d´ Arc, ca. 1928, Solid Bronze, bronze, 3½", Solid Bronze, rarity 5, $90.00.

Plate 88. Umbrella Girls, ca. 1925, X-1, gray metal, 5", #62, rarity 4, $225.00. Other finishes, including bronze, brown, yellow, gold, have been seen.

Plate 89. Ski Queen, ca. 1932, K&O, gray metal, 6½", shopmark, rarity 5*, $175.00.

Plate 90. Curtseying Girl, ca. 1920, bronze, 5½", Austria, rarity 5*, $500.00

Plate 91. Little Red Riding Hood, 1924, Ronson, gray metal, 5", LV Aronson, 1924, rarity 5*, $350.00.

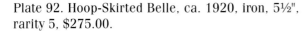

Plate 92. Hoop-Skirted Belle, ca. 1920, iron, 5½", rarity 5, $275.00.

Plate 93. Pink Lady, ca. 1943, JB Hirsch, chalk on polished stone base, 5½", JBH, rarity 5, $125.00.

Plate 94. Girl with Purse, ca. 1926, gray metal with celluloid face, 4¾", rarity 4, $135.00.

Plate 95. Wait Here, ca. 1926, gray metal and celluloid face and fan, on marble base, rarity 5, $275.00.

Plate 96. Curtsy, ca. 1926, gray metal with celluloid face, on marble base, rarity 4, $200.00.

Plate 97. Woman on Couch, ca. 1930, JB Hirsch, gray metal with celluloid face, 4¾", marked JBH, rarity 5, $300.00.

James McNeill Whistler

James McNeill Whistler (1834 – 1903), though American born, spent part of his childhood in Russia since his father served as a civil engineer for the St. Petersburg-to-Moscow railroad. He briefly attended West Point, but was dismissed and moved to Paris to begin his life as an artist, finally choosing London as a settling place.

Whistler's 1875 painting "Nocturne in Black and Gold: The Falling Rocket" was described by critic John Ruskin as "flinging a pot of paint in the public's face." Whistler filed a libel suit in response to this, which he won, but costs of which bankrupted him, prompting a move to Venice in response to the offer of a commission from the fine art society there. Whistler never returned to the U.S. and only after his death was there any show of his work here.

The painting we know as "Whistler's Mother" was originally known as "Arrangement in Grey and Black: Portrait of the Painter's Mother", and was painted in oil on canvas in 1871. Whistler spent about three months in 1871 painting his 67-year-old mother, Anna Matilda McNeill Whistler. Originally, the work was one with Mrs. Whistler standing, but after she tired, her son accommodated a sitting position. The painting is permanently displayed at the Musee d'Orsay in Paris.

Plate 98. Whistler's Mother, ca. 1932, JB Hirsch, gray metal with celluloid face, on marble base, 6½", rarity 4, $225.00.

Plate 98A. Different finish.

Plate 98B. Similar to the two previous Whistlers, this piece is made of plaster, produced appoximately 10 years after the original, but from the same molds. Rarity 5, $150.00.

Plate 99. Spinning Wheel, ca. 1925, attr. JB Hirsch, gray metal with celluloid face, on polished stone base, 6½", rarity 5, $300.00.

Plate 100. Blenko Girl, ca. 1970, Blenko, 8", rarity 3, $40.00.

Plate 101. Goosegirl, ca. 1934, Frankart, gray metal, 5¼", shopmark, rarity 5, $195.00.

Plate 102. Dutch Treat, ca. 1928, iron, 6½", rarity 2, $45.00.

Plate 103. Basket Case, ca. 1930, attr. Armor Bronze, bronze clad, approx. 5½", rarity 4, $125.00.

Plate 104. Nouveau Girls, ca. 1920, Judd, gray metal, approx. 5", rarity 4, $110.00.

Plate 105. FDR Bust, 1933, Ronson, gray metal, approx. 3", Franklin D. Roosevelt, JS 1933 AMW, rarity 5, $110.00. (Collection of Richard Weinstein)

Plate 106. The Aviator, ca. 1928, Connecticut Foundry, bronze or iron, 6", shopmark, The Aviator, rarity 5* bronze, rarity 4 iron, bronze $225.00, iron $125.00. (This piece is cast generally in iron, as are all Connecticut Foundry pieces. The lack of detail and wear on the lettering would suggest that this particular example has been produced from an iron original.)

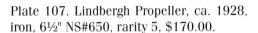

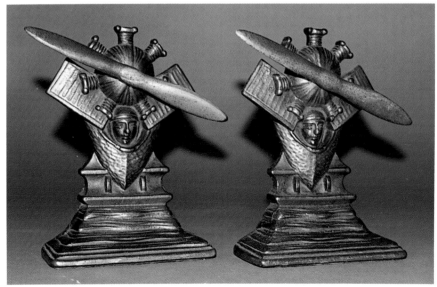

Plate 107. Lindbergh Propeller, ca. 1928, iron, 6½" NS#650, rarity 5, $170.00.

Plate 108. Lindy, ca. 1928, Verona, iron, 6",
shopmark, rarity 4, $110.00.

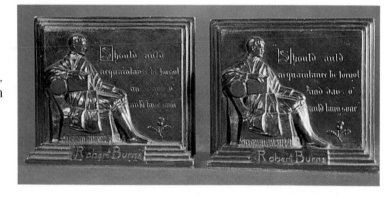

Plate 109. Auld Lang Syne, 1926, K&O, gray metal,
4¾", shopmark, rarity 5, $110.00. (Piece pictured in
AC Becken Jewelers catalog, 1926.)

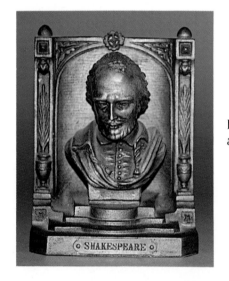

Plate 110. Shakespeare Shrine, ca. 1925, Bradley
and Hubbard, iron, 4", shopmark, rarity 5, $175.00.

Plate 111. Dickens, ca. 1929, Jennings Brothers,
gray metal, 6¼", shopmark, #2062, rarity 5*,
$165.00.

Plate 112. John Harvard, ca. 1928, Jennings Brothers, gray metal, 7", marked Daniel C. French, #2654, rarity 5*, $275.00.

Plate 113. Three Musketeers, ca. 1930, Jennings Brothers, gray metal, 5¾", shopmark, rarity 5, $275.00.

Plate 114. D'Artagnan, ca. 1928, KBV Art Bronze, bronze clad, 7¾", rarity 5*, $225.00. (Courtesy Jay Mendlovitz)

Plate 115. Huck Finn, ca. 1930, Armor Bronze, bronze clad, 7¾", rarity 5, $150.00.

Plate 116. Pan, ca. 1935, Marion Bronze, bronze clad, 7½", shopmark, rarity 5, $175.00.

Plate 117. Minute Man, ca. 1930, Jennings Brothers, gray metal, 9", JB 1755, rarity 5, $175.00.

Plate 118. Town Crier, ca. 1965, PM Craftsman, gray metal, 7¼", company tag, rarity 2, $50.00.

Plate 119. Miles Standish, ca. 1930, gray metal, 7", rarity 5*, $125.00.

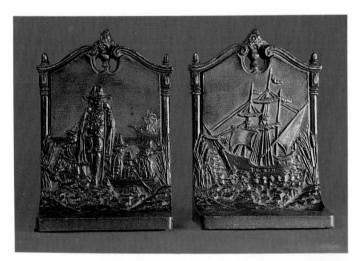

Plate 120. Pilgrim Landing, ca. 1925, Bradley and Hubbard, iron, 5½", shopmark, company tag with legend, rarity 5, $175.00.

Plate 121. Cornell Flux, ca. 1950, Cornell Flux, aluminum, approx. 4", rarity 5, $35.00.

The Puritan

The first Puritans to establish the Massachusetts Bay Company left England in 1629. Five ships, including the Mayflower, brought them to Salem, Massachusetts. Unlike the Pilgrims, who had endured difficult travel, an influenza break, and other privations, the Puritans arrived well stocked to build comfortable homes and lives. In March, 1630, 1,500 Puritan settlers arrived in 11 ships. Many of these were wealthy, owning their own ships and trading companies. This is in stark contrast to the impoverished band of Plymouth settlers, the Pilgrims. The Puritans were motivated to intertwine Church and State. In 1631 a law was passed insisting that membership in an approved church was a requirement for voting privileges. The Pilgrims had determined the exact opposite path, that church and government were to be separate.

Reportedly, Puritans were intolerant of Catholics, Indians, Quakers, and others with dissenting opinions. Representative of this desire for control, five years later an order was passed: "No person householder, or other, shall spend his time idely, or unprofitable under paine of such punishment as the Court shall think meete to inflict." On Sunday, walking or running was forbidden, unless it was to church. Anyone caught kissing in a woman in public, even his own wife, was flogged.

The Puritan is extraordinarily close to the Pilgrim, a large bronze statue by Augustus Saint-Gaudens, in Fairmount Park, Philadelphia, in 1903 – 1904. The primary difference is that the Puritan has a blunderbuss, while the Pilgrim carries a walking stick in its place.

The Puritan was produced first, commissioned by Chester W. Chapin as a monument to Deacon Samuel Chaplin (1595 – 1675). Subsequently, the New England Society of Pennsylvania asked him to make a replica for Philadelphia. Saint-Gaudens's comments on the changes in the figure were: "For the head in the original statue, I used as a model the head of Mr. Chapin, assuming that there would be some family resemblance with the Deacon, who was his direct ancestor. But Mr. Chapin's face is round and Gaelic in character, so in the Philadelphia work, I changed the features completely, giving them the long, New England type, besides altering the folds of the cloak in many respects, the legs, the left hand, and the Bible."

Reference: *Uncommon Clay: The Life and Works of Augustus Saint-Gaudens.* Burke Wilkinson, Harcourt Brace Jovanovich Publishers, 1985.

Plate 122. Puritan, ca. 1924, gray metal, 9¼", rarity 5*, $275.00.

Plate 123. The Village Blacksmith, ca. 1930, bronze, approx. 5½", rarity 4, $125.00. (Also seen in gray metal, rarity 3, $65.00.)

Plate 124. Sir Francis Drake, ca. 1925, Jennings Brothers, gray metal, 3", JB 2310, rarity 4, $50.00.

Plate 125. Sir Galahad, ca. 1923, gray metal, 6½", rarity 5, $125.00. Other finishes seen: bronze.

Plate 126. Galahad in Archway, ca. 1925, iron, 6", rarity 3, $50.00.

Plate 127. Crusaders, ca. 1926, Hubley, iron, 5½", #300, rarity 3, $75.00. (Courtesy Jay Mendlovitz)

Plate 128. Spanish Conquistadors, ca. 1925, solid bronze, bronze, 5", rarity 5*, $300.00.

Plate 129. Atlas, ca. 1940, JB Hirsch, chalk on polished stone base, 7¾", shopmark, rarity 5*, $135.00.

Plate 130. Little Lord Fauntleroy, ca. 1925, gray metal, 8", rarity 5, $150.00.

Plate 131. St. George and the Dragon (Hubley), ca. 1925, Hubley, iron, 5½", #312, rarity 3, $85.00.

Plate 132. St. George and the Dragon (Acorn), ca. 1925, Acorn, bronze, 6½", shopmark, #606, St. George and the Dragon, rarity 5*, $175.00.

Plate 133. Knight Errant, ca. 1925, bronze, 6¼", rarity 4, $95.00.

Plate 134. Knight in Archway, 1931, Gorham, bronze, 8", Gorham; The Traveler's Convention, Palm Beach Florida 1931, rarity 5, $425.00. (This piece is not always marked.)

Plate 135. Asian Warriors, ca. 1930, JB Hirsch (after a piece by Bruno Zach), 7¼", gray metal with celluloid face, on polished stone base, rarity 5, $225.00.

Plate 136. Bazaar Scene, ca. 1920, Austria, gray metal, 6¼", "Austria," rarity 5, $325.00.

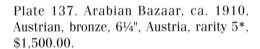

Plate 137. Arabian Bazaar, ca. 1910, Austrian, bronze, 6¼", Austria, rarity 5*, $1,500.00.

Plate 138. Classical Men, ca. 1925, bronze on marble base, 6", rarity 5*, $150.00.

Plate 139. Against The Wall, ca. 1928, Armor Bronze, bronze clad, 9", shopmark, signature A. Mehodon, rarity 5, $165.00.

Plate 140. Sentinel, ca. 1940, polished brass with plastic body and hat, 7¼", shopmark, rarity 4, $275.00. Other finishes seen: black and bronze.

Plate 141. Bending Backwards, ca. 1925, iron, 6", rarity 4, $75.00.

Plate 142. Slashing Samurai, ca.1930, Ronson, gray metal, 7⅛", company tag #14581, rarity 5, $325.00.

Plate 143. Star Climber, ca. 1930, gray metal, 5½", rarity 5*, $225.00.

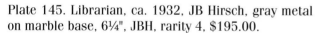

Plate 144. Pioneers, 1925, Pompeian Bronze, gray metal, 4½", Pioneers, Pompeian Bronze, 1925, rarity 5 (polychrome), 4 (bronze finish), $200.00 (polychrome), $165.00 (bronze finish).

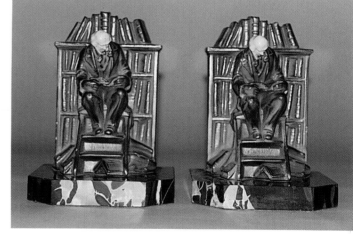

Plate 145. Librarian, ca. 1932, JB Hirsch, gray metal on marble base, 6¼", JBH, rarity 4, $195.00.

Plate 146. Man Reading, ca. 1932, JB Hirsch, chalk on polished stone base, (made in several finishes) 4½", JBH, RUHL (Artist J. Ruhl, b. 1873) rarity 4, $125.00.

Plate 147. Hold Those Books, ca. 1932, JB Hirsch, gray metal on polished stone base, 7", rarity 4, $195.00.

Plate 148. Asleep at Mid-Story, ca. 1929, K&O, gray metal, shopmark, 4¼", rarity 4, $165.00.

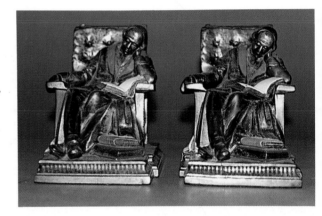

Plate 149. Bookworm, 1931, Nuart, 6¾", gray metal, shopmark (very faint), NYC, rarity 4, $135.00. (The description of this bookend, in the 1931 catalog reproduction reprinted by Art Deco By Design, P.O. Box 1321, Dearborn, Michigan 48121-1321, reads: "Book Worm Bookends. Here no doubt we have the most appropriate of bookends. A rare combination of humor and dignity that should be appreciated by every connoisseur of books." Originally priced at $3.00 per pair.)

Plate 150. Student Monk, 1926, K&O, gray metal, 7", shopmark, rarity 4, $150.00.

Plate 151. Study, ca. 1925, iron, 5½", #42, rarity 4, $125.00.

Plate 152. Library Monk, 1920, Ronson, gray metal, LV Aronson, 1920, rarity 4, $125.00.

Plate 153. Gnome in Library, ca. 1924, Bradley and Hubbard, iron, 5", rarity 5, $195.00.

Plate 154. Servant of Knowledge, ca. 1930, attr. JB Hirsch, gray metal on polished stone base, 5", rarity 5*, $250.00.

Plate 155. Student, ca. 1925, attr. Judd, iron, 6", #9741, rarity 4, $175.00; in expandable rack form, rarity 4, $150.00.

Plate 156. Deep in Thought, ca. 1925, attr. JB Hirsch, gray metal on polished stone base, 6", J Ruhl, rarity 5*, $275.00.

Plate 157. Turbanned Scholar, 1923, Ronson, gray metal, 3¼", LV Aronson 1923, rarity 5 (polychrome), 3 (other finishes), $110.00 (polychrome), $65.00 (other finishes).

Plate 158. Father Knickerbocker, ca. 1925, attr. Judd, iron, 5¾", #9936, company tag "Father Knickerbocker," rarity 5, $175.00.

Plate 159. Roman Scribe, ca. 1922, Pompeian Bronze, bronze clad, 7", Pompeian Bronze, rarity 4, $150.00.

Plate 160. Thinker (Gift House), 1928, Gift House, iron, 5¾", shopmark, 1928, #D-51, rarity 5, $125.00.

Plate 161. Three Graduates, ca. 1932, K&O, gray metal, shopmark, rarity 5, $110.00.

Plate 162. Think Figuratively, ca. 1925, Ronson, gray metal, 6", company tag #11375, rarity 4, $100.00.

Plate 163. The Thinker, ca.1930, Ronson, gray metal, 5½", company tag #11237, rarity 4, $125.00.

Plate 164. The Thinker, ca. 1928, Hubley, iron, 5", rarity 2, $35.00.

Plate 165. Greek Athlete, ca. 1927, Ronson, gray metal on marbelized gray metal base, 5½", company tag #11945M, rarity 5, $300.00.

Plate 166. Blacksmith, ca.1925, Littco, iron, 5", rarity 5, $175.00.

Plate 167. American Chain Company, ca. 1930, gray metal, approx. 4½", this piece unmarked, but identical piece seen with logo "American Chain Company," rarity 5, $95.00.

Plate 168. Pirate, ca. 1925, gray metal on marble base, 6½", rarity 4, $225.00. (This same figure has been seen on a variety of marble and metal structures, on a jewelry box, lamps, etc., and portrayed in chalk as well.)

Plate 169. Checking the Treasure, ca. 1930, attr. Armor Bronze, bronze clad, 5¼", rarity 4, $95.00. (Collection of Sue Benoliel)

Plate 170. Pirate with Chest, ca. 1928, Littco, iron, 5¼", rarity 4, $80.00.

Plate 171 Pirate Booty, ca. 1925, Hubley, iron, 4¾", rarity 3, $65.00.

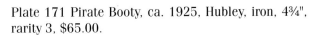

Plate 172. Swashbuckler, ca. 1940, Dodge, gray metal, 7¾", copyright Paul Herzl, shopmark, rarity 5, $110.00.

Plate 173. Pirate Stands Alone, ca. 1928, Littco, iron, 7", rarity 4, $110.00. (Same figure in gray metal, various makers, rarity 3, $65.00.)

Plate 174. Buccaneer, 1930, Connecticut Foundry, iron, 7¼", shopmark, Buccaneer, 1930, rarity 5, $125.00.

Plate 175. Pirate's Booty, ca. 1925, Littco, iron, 6½", rarity 3, $75.00. (Collection of Sue Benoliel)

Plate 176. Soldier with Sabre, ca. 1931, attr. JB Hirsch, gray metal on polished stone base with celluloid face and knee, 8¼", rarity 5, $275.00.

Plate 177. The Cavalier, ca. 1928, attr. Armor Bronze, 5½", bronze clad, signed Paul Hertzel, rarity 5*, $125.00. (Collection of Sue Benoliel)

Plate 178. The Little Prince, ca. 1960, gray metal, 7½", rarity 3, $65.00.

Plate 179. Roundup, ca. 1945, gray metal, 6", Phil Goodan, rarity 5*, $165.00.

Plate 180. Fisherman with Net, ca. 1928, Littco, iron, 6¾", rarity 4, $175.00.

Plate 181. Friar, ca. 1928, Littco, iron, 5", rarity 5, $215.00 (polychrome), $190.00 (bronze finish).

Plate 182. Policeman, ca. 1925, attr. Littco, iron, 6¾", rarity 5*, $250.00.

Plate 183. Camel Driver, ca. 1926, iron, 6", rarity 5, $150.00.

Plate 184. The Bedouin, ca. 1925, Hubley, iron, 5¾", rarity 4 (polychrome), 3 (other finishes), $125.00 (polychrome), $95.00 (other finishes). (Collection of Sue Benoliel)

Plate 185. Roman and Scroll, ca. 1932, K&O, gray metal, 5¼", shopmark, "J. Ruhl" (artist John Ruhl, born 1873). $110.00. Also seen in polychrome, $130.00.

Plate 186. Tom & Huck, ca. 1925, Bradley and Hubbard, iron, 7", shopmark, rarity 5*, $300.00.

Plate 187. Profanity, 1928, Connecticut Foundry, iron, 6", shopmark, 1928, rarity 5*, $175.00.

Plate 188. Pushing Men, ca. 1920, Gorham, bronze, 6¼", shopmark, Isidore Konti, Sc., rarity 5*, $3,000.00.

Plate 189. Gladiators, ca. 1932, bronze on marble base, 7¾", rarity 5*, $600.00.

Plate 190. Charioteer, ca. 1925, attr. JB Hirsch, gray metal on polished stone base, 5", rarity 5*, $275.00.

Plate 191. Swimmer, ca. 1946, attr. Dodge, gray metal, 5¾", rarity 4, $85.00.

Plate 192. Ski Jump, ca. 1928, WB, gray metal, 7½", shopmark, rarity 5*, $175.00.

Plate 193. Football Player, ca. 1925, Hubley, iron, 5½", rarity 5, $175.00.

Plate 194. Discus Thrower, ca. 1928, Littco, iron, 7", rarity 3, $110.00.

Plate 195. Golf, ca. 1930, Jennings Brothers, gray metal, approx. 14", shopmark, rarity 5*, $350.00.

Plate 196. Golfer, ca. 1930, Ronson, gray metal, 6½", rarity 5, $175.00.

COUPLES

The Pioneer Woman is a bronze statue of a mother wearing a sunbonnet, carrying a book in one hand, and leading her son with the other. In the late 1920s, Ernest Whitworth Marland, an oil man, U.S. Congressman, and 10th governor of Oklahoma, invited 12 of the leading sculptors of the world to submit designs for a competition. Invited sculptors were Bryant Baker, A. Stirling Calder, Jo Davidson, James Fraser (sculptor of "End of the Trail" and designer of the buffalo nickel), John Gregor, F. Lynn Jenkins, Mario Korbel, Arthur Lee, H.A. MacNeil, Maurice Sterne, Mahonri Young, and Wheeler Williams. Additional sculptors, including two women, had been invited, but declined: Mrs. A.V.H. Huntington, Mrs. Gertrude Vanderbilt Whitney, George Grey Barnard, Daniel Chester French (designer of Lincoln in the Lincoln Memorial), and Paul Manship. The sculpture was to commemorate the heroic women that braved the hardships of daily life as pioneer women. The 12 submitted sculptures (each artist received a $2,500 commission for his work) were each 33 inches tall, and were sent on a tour of major American cities, beginning with the Reinhardt Galleries on February 26, 1927. Bryant Baker was paid $50,000 for his winning sculpture, which captured the majority of the 750,000 votes cast.

Bryant Baker was born in London, England, in 1881 and graduated from the Royal Academy of Arts. Baker began his sculpting career with a post as foreman-sculptor at the Victoria and Albert Museum in London, and came to the U.S. in 1916. He served as a sergeant in the U.S. Army 1918 – 1919. On April 22, 1930, Will Rogers gave the principal address at the dedication unveiling of the 17-foot-high-statue. This particular date was chosen because it commemorated the anniversary of the first "run" for land in Oklahoma. Herbert Hoover gave a radio address heard in person by the 40,000 in attendance. A minor earthquake cracked the base of the statue in 1952, but after a 1978 repair, Will Rogers Jr. came for the rededication.

The Pioneer Woman statue is currently located on 14.5 acres adjacent to the Pioneer Woman Museum in Ponca City, Oklahoma, which was constructed in 1958. The 12,000 pound statue has a 13' base, bringing the total height to 30'. The statue was dedicated to pioneer women with the following inscription on its base: "In appreciation of the heroic character of the women who braved the dangers and endured the hardships incident to the daily life of the pioneer and homesteader in this country."

Pioneer Women bookends (Jennings Brothers, manufacturers) are rare. The detail is excellent, and the base is signed by the artist. Several finishes have been seen, including bronze, chocolate brown, and green-bronze patina.

References: Pioneer Woman Statue Museum, Ponca City, Okla.

Jan Prough, *Ponca City News*, Sunday, September 12, 1993, page 2

Plate 197. Dutch Pair, ca. 1925, Ronson, gray metal, 5½", company tag #16510, rarity 5 (polychrome), 4 (other finishes), $175.00 (polychrome), $125.00 (other finishes).

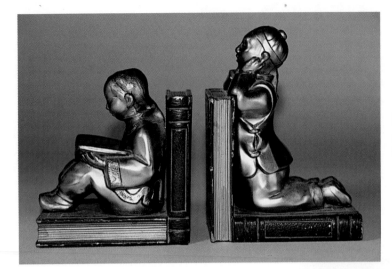

Plate 198. Chinese Students, ca. 1930, Ronson, gray metal, 5¼", company tag #16138, rarity 3, $95.00.

Plate 198A. Different base and finish, note "quilted fabric" detail, rarity 5, $135.00.

Plate 198B. Different base, rarity 4, $110.00.

Plate 198C. Polychrome, rarity 5, $135.00.

Plate 199. One of Us Was Studying, ca. 1930, Ronson, gray metal, 9", company tag #12552, rarity 3, $150.00.

Plate 200. Angelus Call to Prayer, ca. 1925, K&O, gray metal, shopmark, rarity 4, $125.00.

Plate 201. Millet Scenes, 1916, Griffoul Foundry, bronze, 5", shopmark, signed by sculptor on obverse (Lambert), dated 1916, rarity 5*, $225.00.

Plate 202. Angelus (Hubley), ca. 1925, Hubley, iron, approx. 5½", rarity 3, $65.00.

Jean Francois Millet

    Millet (October 4, 1814 – January 20, 1875) captured the attention of sculptors with his noteworthy portrayals of peasant life in oil. He was raised in Normandy, France, by farmer parents, and studied painting in Cherbourg until the age of 20. Although Millet had an express preference for the countryside, he studied under Paul Delaroche in Paris until 1849, at which time he moved to the Fontainbleau forest, the small village of Barbizon.

    Millet is credited with bringing a grace and dignity previously not attained to simple lifestyles and peasant scenes. His painting "The Gleaners", depicted in Plate 204, and "Angelus Call To Prayer," Plate 203, are both familiar to art lovers. The Angelus was painted in 1857 – 1859, and now is in the Louvre, Paris.

Plate 203. Angelus Call to Prayer (CF), 1928, Connecticut Foundry, iron, 5½", Angelus Call to Prayer, rarity 3, $55.00.

Plate 204. The Gleaners, ca. 1925, K&O, gray metal, shopmark, 4¼", rarity 4, $125.00.

Plate 205. Pancho Villa And Sancho, ca. 1960, stone/resin composite, WW, rarity 5*, $125.00.

Plate 206A. Reverse markings from Plate 206.

Plate 206. Alden and Priscilla, 1928, Connecticut Foundry, iron, 5", shopmark, Alden and Priscilla, 1928, one pair is marked Connecticut Foundry, the other has only shopmark, rarity 4, $75.00.

Plate 207. John Alden and Priscilla (B&H), ca. 1925, Bradley and Hubbard, iron, 5¾", shopmark, rarity 4, $150.00.

Plate 208. Victorian Couple, ca. 1925, Judd, iron, 6", shopmark, #9662, rarity 4, $85.00.

Plate 209. Colonial Trio, ca. 1925, iron, 5", rarity 3, $50.00.

Plate 210. Pocahontas and Smith, ca. 1929, bronze, 5¾", rarity 5, $175.00.

Plate 211. Colonial Couple, ca. 1925, bronze, 6", rarity 5*, $275.00.

Plate 212. Madonna and Child, ca. 1925, Verona, iron, 6¾", Verona, rarity 5*, $150.00.

Plate 213. Holy Mother and Child, 1924 (copyright #73078 registered to Olga Popoff Muller, December 1, 1924, of Snead & Co), Snead Ironworks, iron, 4¾", shopmark, rarity 4, $60.00.

Plate 214. Pioneer Woman, 1927, Jennings Brothers, gray metal, 8½", JB 8355, Bryant Baker, rarity 5, $300.00.

Plate 215. French Children, ca. 1920, gray metal, 8", rarity 5*, $600.00.

Plate 216. Dutch boy and girl, windmill pictured in background, ca. 1925, Albany Foundry, iron, 5", rarity 5, $110.00. Also seen in polychrome.

Plate 217. Read to Me, ca. 1925, X-1, gray metal, 5½", #509, $125.00.

Plate 217A. Polychrome, rarity 5, $175.00.

Plate 218. Wedding Children, ca. 1934, Nuart, gray metal, 5½", shopmark, rarity 4, $90.00.

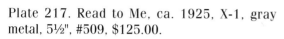

Plate 219. Field and Riley, ca. 1925, Bradley and Hubbard, iron, 5½", shopmark, rarity 4, $95.00.

Plate 220. Dutch Boy and Girl, ca. 1934, Frankart, 5½", gray metal, shopmark, rarity 5, $150.00.

Plate 221. Woman and Child, ca. 1922, Pompeian Bronze, bronze clad, 6½", rarity 5, $165.00.

Plate 222. Intertwined Couple, ca. 1929, bronze, 5", rarity 5*, $210.00.

Plate 223. This Is a Date?, ca. 1930, Frankart, gray metal, 5½", shopmark, rarity 4, $125.00.

Plate 224. Men at Her Feet, ca. 1925, bronze, approx 6½", rarity 5, $125.00. (Courtesy Warren and Dolores Wilkinson, Wilkinson Antiques)

Plate 225. Deco Kiss, ca. 1927, attr. JB Hirsch, gray metal on polished stone base, 6¾", rarity 5*, $375.00.

Plate 226. Harlequin Pair, ca. 1985, pottery, 11½", rarity 4, $65.00. These are actually empty Chianti bottles, and do well filled with water and corked to provide weight and stability.

Plate 227. Pirate Couple, ca. 1932, K&O, gray metal, 10½", rarity 4, $175.00.

Plate 228. Robin and Marian, ca. 1924, JB Hirsch, gray metal on polished stone base, 7", rarity 5, $295.00.

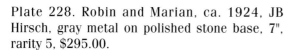

Plate 229. Tryst, ca. 1924 , Hubley, iron, 5½", #301, rarity 3, $75.00.

Plate 230. Cupid and Psyche, ca. 1928, X-1, gray metal, 4½", #501, rarity 5*, $135.00.

Plate 231. Ruling Couple, ca. 1980, Bellinni, 7", company tag "Bellini, Italy," rarity 5, $110.00.

Plate 232. Adoration, 1923, Pompeian Bronze, gray metal, 6½", Adoration, PB, 1923, rarity 4, $175.00.

Plate 233. Dante and Beatrice, Rock-hewn, ca. 1925, Jennings Brothers, gray metal, 6¼", shopmark, #2434, rarity 4, $150.00.

Plate 234. Dante and Beatrice (Ronson), ca. 1923, Ronson, gray metal, 6", company tag #16518/16519, rarity 4, $175.00.

Plate 234A. Ronson shopmark.

Plate 235. Dante and Beatrice (AB), ca. 1925, Armor Bronze, gray metal, 6¾", Armor Bronze, rarity 5*, $175.00. Note: This is the only piece I have seen to date made by Armor Bronze that is made not in the bronze clad (weighted bronze) style, but cast gray metal. The company name is embossed on the rear of the piece.

Plate 236. Dante and Beatrice Books, ca. 1935, Jennings Brothers, gray metal, 6", JB Pat Appl. For, rarity 4, $195.00.

Plate 237. Dante's Inferno, ca. 1925, JB Hirsch, gray metal with celluloid face and hands, on polished stone base, 8½", J Ruhl, rarity 5, $225.00.

Plate 238. Dante, 1930, Connecticut Foundry, iron, 5¾", shopmark, Dante Alighieri, 1930, rarity 4, $85.00.

Plate 240. Dante Shrine (K&O), ca. 1925, K&O, gray metal, shopmark, 6⅛", rarity 5, $175.00.

Plate 241. Dante Shrine (MB), ca. 1925, Millers Brass Foundry, brass, 6⅛", shopmark, rarity 5*, $195.00.

LINCOLN

Lincoln is ostensibly the most frequently represented individual in bookend art. Some of the most well-known sculptures of Lincoln were executed by Leonard Wells Volk, Daniel Chester French, Thomas D. Jones, Gutzon Borglum, Augustus Saint-Gaudens, and George Grey Barnard. Indeed, Lincoln has been called "the most sculpted man in history."

Surprisingly, early portraiture of Lincoln was notoriously unsuccessful, and shortly after his nomination for the presidency, his secretary, John C. Nicolay, reported that the attempted artistic results were "...no more like the man as the grain of sand to the mountain..." What some regard as the most successful of all Lincoln studies was the work of Leonard Wells Volk. Volk got Lincoln to agree to make a plaster cast of his face, which would then be used to make a bust. Two years later, the process is reported to have been done by applying cold wet plaster to Lincoln's face, with straws inserted into his nostrils to permit breathing. About two months later, Volk sought to make plaster casts of Lincoln's hands, and received consent, qualified by Lincoln that his right hand was unnaturally puffy due to swelling from his prolific shaking of hands done the night before with post-nomination well-wishers.

Augustus Saint-Gaudens's bronze statue "Lincoln the Man" was placed in Chicago's Lincoln Park in 1887. A Gutzon Borglum marble bust of Lincoln was given to the Capitol in 1908 by Eugene Meyer, Jr. and is housed in the Rotunda. Later, in 1911, Borglum had his "Seated Lincoln on a Bench" (Plate 244) placed in Newark, New Jersey. In 1937, Borglum created the massive mountainside face of Lincoln at Mt. Rushmore.

A popular portrait, "Lincoln and his son Tad," was painted by Franklin Courter, and is housed in the office of the Senate Minority Leader in the U.S. Capitol.

Reference: "The Many Faces of Lincoln," Harold Holzer, *The Antique Trader*, April, 12, 1995.

Compilation of Works of Art and Other Objects in the United States Capitol, United States Government Printing Office, Washington, D.C., 1965.

Plate 242. Borglum's Lincoln, 1931, Ronson, gray metal, 4½", company tag #14149, rarity 4, $90.00. (Also comes in 5½", company tag #16561, and 6½", company tag #16250.)

Plate 243. French's Lincoln, ca. 1924, Gift House, Inc., iron, 6", D 57, NYC, rarity 5, $195.00.

Plate 244. Seated Lincoln (Nuart), 1924, Nuart, gray metal, 6½", shopmark, 1924, rarity 4, $110.00.

Plate 245. Lincoln's Cabin, ca. 1925, Judd, iron, 3¾", rarity 3, $50.00.

Plate 246. Lincoln at Gettysburg, ca. 1930, K&O, gray metal, 7¾", Lincoln at Gettsyburg, rarity 5*, $225.00. Reissue by PMC, post 1964 also seen, rarity 4, $75.00.

Plate 247. Lincoln's Monument, ca. 1930, WB, approx. 5½", bronze, shopmark, rarity 4, $150.00. (Courtesy John Asfor)

Plate 247A. Showing WB shopmark on reverse.

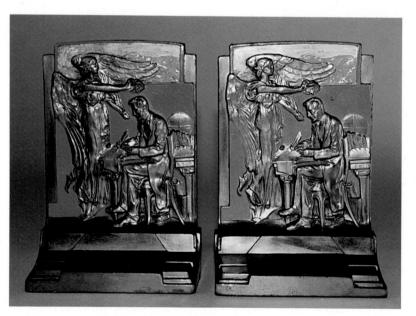

Plate 248. The Great Emancipator, 1925, Pompeian Bronze, gray metal, 5½", The Emancipator PB & Co., 1925, rarity 5, $225.00.

Plate 249. French's Lincoln, ca. 1925, Jennings Brothers, gray metal, 7", rarity 4, $250.00.

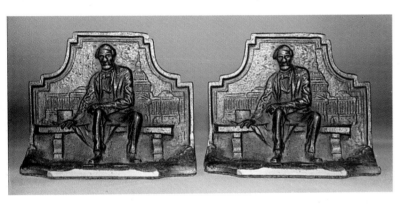

Plate 250. Seated Lincoln, ca. 1930, Solid Bronze, bronze, Solid Bronze, 3¾", rarity 3, $90.00.

Plate 251. Lincoln Medallion, 1921, Ronson, gray metal, 4¾", LV Aronson, 1921, rarity 3, $90.00. (Collection of Richard Weinstein)

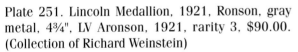

Plate 252. Lincoln Bust, ca. 1928 (appears in 1928 Sears catalog), Verona, iron, approx. 6½", shopmark, rarity 3, $65.00.

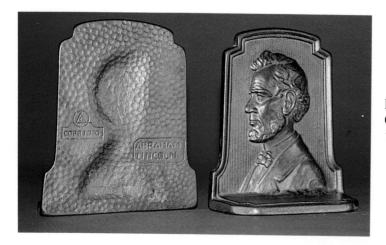

Plate 253. Lincoln Profile (CF), 1930, Connecticut Foundry, iron, 6", Lincoln, 1930, shopmark, rarity 4, $95.00

Plate 254. Lincoln Profile, ca. 1926, attr. Judd, iron, 5½", #9747, rarity 4, $95.00.

Plate 255. Lincoln Profile, ca. 1925, iron, 5¼", rarity 3, $65.00. (Courtesy Jay Mendlovitz)

Plate 256. Lincoln and Tad, ca. 1925, iron, approx. 7", rarity 4, $110.00.

# WASHINGTON

Although not as popularly represented in bookend art as Lincoln, George Washington is often found. "Washington Crossing the Delaware" is shown in Plate 257. The original painting by Emmanuel Gottlied Leutze (1816 – 68) was created in Dusseldorf, Germany, in 1851. Leutze began his painting in 1848, using American visitors as models, but unfortunately the original was severely damaged by fire in 1850. The scene depicts Christmas night, 1776.

Plate 257. Washington Crossing the Delaware, ca. 1932, K&O, gray metal, 6¾", shopmark, rarity 4 (polychrome) 3 (bronze finish), $175.00 (polychrome), $125.00 (bronze finish).

Plate 258. Washington Bust (Ronson), 1932, Ronson, gray metal, 5½", Art Metal Works, 1932, rarity 4, $85.00. (Collection of Richard Weinstein)

Plate 259. President General, ca. 1925, Hubley, bronze, 5¼", #234, artist signed "Allen" to the right of Horse's Forefoot, rarity 4 (bronze) 3 (iron), $150.00 (bronze), $75.00 (iron).

Plate 260. Washington Bust, ca. 1920, iron, rarity 4, $75.00.

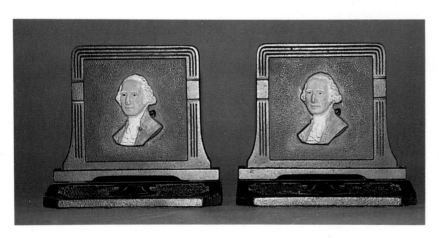

Plate 261. George Washington, ca. 1926, attr. Judd, iron, 5½", #9679, rarity 4, $85.00.

NATIVE AMERICANS

The End of the Trail

This statue was sculpted by James Earle Fraser (1876 – 1953) for the 1915 Panama Pacific Exposition in San Francisco. It is intended to represent the ultimate defeat of the American Indian. This work won the exposition's gold medal, and became an overnight success in the popular media. Fraser had intended the statue be placed on Presidio Point overlooking San Francisco Bay, but the imminence of World War I and scarcity of metal doomed the bronze casting project. The statue was put in storage until brought out and placed in Mooney Grove Park (near Visalia, California) in 1918. In 1968 the National Cowboy Hall of Fame (Oklahoma City) negotiated possession of the statue in exchange for a bronze casting of the statue to replace the original. Leonard McMurry of Oklahoma City and Cesare Contini of New York City completed the restoration of the figure and created molds for the bronze casting which resides in Mooney Grove Park today (having been placed there on December 19, 1971).

Although this dramatic 18' statue is well known by everyone, it is often mislabeled as being done by Remington, and referred to by a variety of inaccurate titles, e.g., "The Final Defeat," "The Last Trail," etc. (See Plates 262 and 263.) There are at least 20 different versions of this statue seen in bookend art; most are lacking the grace and beauty of the Indian and his animal, and are inaccurate to detail. Often the spear and other items are missing.

Although Fraser was quite famous in the early 1900s, his name is rarely heard today. He is also the designer of the buffalo nickel, but since these are out of circulation (since 1938, when they were replaced with the Jefferson nickel) only coin collectors and folks over 40 recognize the artwork.

Plate 262. End of the Trail (CF), 1928, Connecticut Foundry, iron, 5", shopmark, "The Last Trail," rarity 3, $50.00.

Plate 263. End of the Trail, ca. 1930, Ronson, gray metal, 6", company tag #11478, rarity 4 (polychrome), 3 (other finishes), $110.00 (polychrome), $95.00 (other finishes).

Cyrus Edwin Dallin

Cyrus Edwin Dallin (1861 – 1944) was born in Springville, Utah. He began his sculpting interests while working in a mine, run by his father, using local clay. Patrons recognized his talent, and sponsored his study under Ruman H. Bartlett in Boston, Massachusetts; Henri Chapu in Paris, France, 1888 – 1890, and Jean Dampt, Paris, 1896 – 1899.

Dallin achieved great acclaim during his lifetime, winning prizes at the Louisiana Purchase Exhibition, the 1904 St Louis World's Fair, and the 1915 San Franciso Panama-Pacific International Exposition.

Probably his most famous piece is "Appeal to the Great Spirit," a 1912 bronze work which stands in front of the Museum of Fine Arts in Boston, Massachusetts; a miniature version adorns the office of President Bill Clinton. This sculpture was the final of four pieces dedicated to the fate of the Native American: "The Signal of Peace" (1890) is in Lincoln Park Chicago; "The Medicine Man" (1899) is in Fairmount Park, Philadelphia; "The Protest" (1904) was never cast as a monumental bronze piece.

Plate 264. Appeal to the Great Spirit (CT), ca. 1925, CT, iron, 6½", shopmark, rarity 5, $95.00.

Plate 265. The Appeal to the Great Spirit (CF), 1929, Connecticut Foundry, iron, 5¾", shopmark, Appeal to the Great Spirit, 1929, rarity 4, $85.00.

Plate 266. Appeal to the Great Spirit (CED), ca. 1926, gray metal, 7¼", markings CED (initials of sculptor, Cyrus Edwin Dallin). With the exception of the artist's initials, this piece is identical to Plate 267.

Plate 267. Appeal to the Great Spirit, ca. 1926, gray metal, 7¼", rarity 4, $195.00.

Plate 268. Indian Scout, ca. 1927, Jennings Brothers, gray metal, 5", JB 1927, rarity 4, $170.00.

Plate 269. Search the Plain, ca. 1925, Ronson, gray metal, 6½", company tag #16505, rarity 5*, $225.00.

Plate 270. One Feather, ca. 1928, Z-R, iron 6¼", shopmark, #44, rarity 4, $125.00.

Plate 271. Indian Brave, ca. 1926, attr. Judd, iron, 5", 9964, rarity 4, $175.00. (Also comes as expandable.)

Plate 272. Indian Chief, ca. 1926, iron, 5", rarity 4, $75.00.

Plate 273. Adorned Indian, ca. 1923, Ronson, gray metal, 5¾", AMW, Newark, NJ (on underside of base, may be underneath felt covering), rarity 5*, $400.00.

Plate 274. Sitting Bull, ca. 1924, brass, 6¾",
rarity 5, $275.00. (Collection of John Asfor)

Plate 275. Full Headdress, ca. 1928, Judd,
iron, 5", rarity 4, $190.00.(Collection of Sue
Benoliel)

Plate 276. Hiawatha, ca. 1925, Bradley and
Hubbard, bronze, 6¼", shopmark, rarity 5,
$275.00. (Courtesy Jay Mendlovitz)

Plate 277. Indian Maiden's Bowl, ca. 1930, copper clad, approx. 5", rarity 5, $125.00 (Courtesy
Kay Ross's White Elephant Antiques, Dallas)

Plate 278. Indian with Spear, ca. 1926, Jennings Brothers, gray metal, 5", shopmark #1699, rarity 5, $325.00.

Plate 279. Indian Lancer, ca. 1926, Jennings Brothers, gray metal, 5", shopmark, #1996, rarity 5, $225.00.

Plate 280. Awaiting the Prey, ca. 1935, K&O, gray metal, 6¾", shopmark, rarity 5 (polychrome) 4 (other finishes), $215.00 (polychrome), $165.00 (other finishes).

Plate 281. Indian Potter, ca. 1925, Littco, iron, 4½", rarity 4, $135.00. Also seen in polychrome, bronze, and copper flashed.

Plate 282. Cleared Path, ca. 1928, bronze, 6¾",
A. Dloumy, rarity 5*, $225.00. (Collection of
Sue Benoliel)

Plate 283. Birchbark Trip, Ronson, gray metal,
5½", rarity 5, $225.00.

Plate 284. In Pursuit, 1924, Ronson, gray
metal, approx. 4", LV Aronson, 1924, rarity 4,
$110.00. (Collection of Richard Weinstein)

Plate 285. Indian Archer, ca. 1925, WB,
bronze, 5½", shopmark, rarity 5, $125.00.

BIRDS

Plate 286. Brass Eagle, ca. 1940, attr. Virginia Metalcrafters, brass, 6", VM, rarity 4, $150.00. (Collection of Sue Benoliel)

Plate 287. Tripod Eagle, ca. 1934, Frankart, gray metal, 6¾", shopmark, rarity 4, $135.00.

Plate 288. Eagle Poised, ca. 1925, Bradley and Hubbard, iron, 4½", shopmark, rarity 5, $175.00.

Plate 289. American Eagle, ca. 1925, Bradley and Hubbard, iron, 5¾", shopmark, rarity 4, $80.00.

Plate 290. God Bless America, ca. 1930, Ronson, gray metal, 5½", company tag #16607, rarity 5, $125.00. (Collection of Richard Weinstein)

Plate 291. Heraldic Eagle, ca. 1935, Syroco, Syroco wood, 6", rarity 3, $30.00.

Plate 292. Patriotic Eagle, ca. 1970, coated chalk, approx. 5", rarity 3, $20.00.

Plate 293. Perched Eagle, ca. 1934, gray metal, 7½", rarity 4, $115.00.

Plate 294. Ready for Flight, ca. 1940, Cambridge Glass, 5½", rarity 4, $160.00.

Plate 295. Amber Owl, ca. 1950, Viking, 5", rarity 3, $25.00.

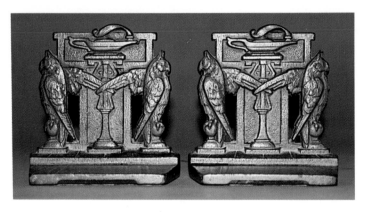

Plate 296. Lamp of Knowledge, ca. 1926, attr. Judd, iron, 4¾", #9886, rarity 4, $100.00.

Plate 297. Night Watchman, 1943, Fostoria, 7½", rarity 5, $350.00. (Collection of Michael Horseman)

Plate 298. Wise Face, ca. 1924, attr. Judd, iron, 6¼", #3773, rarity 5, $160.00.

Plate 299. Wings Astride, 1940 – 1943, Fostoria Glass, rarity 5, $190.00. (Collection of Michael Horseman)

Plate 300. Owl in Archway, ca. 1925, X-1, gray metal, 4¼", #506, rarity 5, $135.00.

Plate 301. Owl in Archway (Fleuron), ca. 1930, Fleuron, Durez resin, Fleuron, North Tonawanda, New York, rarity 5*, $125.00.

Plate 302. Owl Roycroft, ca. 1920, Roycroft, copper, 4¼", shopmark, rarity 3, $110.00. (Courtesy Jay Mendlovitz)

Plate 303. Perched Peacock, ca. 1925, Bradley and Hubbard, iron, shopmark, approx. 6½", rarity 5, $135.00.

Plate 304. Proud Peacock, ca. 1930, X-1, iron, 5¾", #501, rarity 4, $150.00. (Essentially identical piece marketed by Art Metal Works, rarity 5, $195.00, marked AMW.)

Plate 305. Peacock Splendor, ca. 1930, bronze, 5¾", rarity 5, $175.00.

Plate 306. Splendor, ca. 1925, Pompeian Bronze, gray metal, 3¾", Splendor, PB, & Co., rarity 4, $110.00.

Plate 307. Penguin Play, ca. 1933, gray metal, 3½", rarity 5, $110.00.

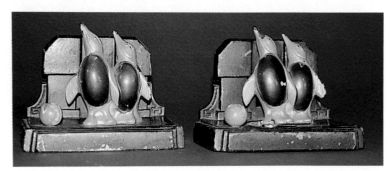

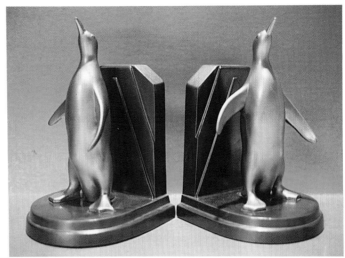

Plate 308. Perfect Penguin, ca. 1930, Ronson, gray metal, 5½", company tag #14773, rarity 5*, $350.00. (Collection of Richard Weinstein)

Plate 309. Proud Penguin, ca. 1930, Frankart, gray metal, 7", shopmark, rarity 5, $300.00. (Collection of Sue Benoliel)

Plate 311. Penguin Family, ca. 1925, gray metal, 4¾", rarity 5*, $225.00.

Plate 310. Big Bird, bronze and ivory, 15", rarity 5*, $7,500.00. (Courtesy of Miami Beach Convention Show)

Plate 313. Bronze Bird, ca. 1920, bronze on marble base, 5", rarity 5*, $400.00.

Plate 312. Swan Design, ca. 1930, Ronson, gray metal, 4¾", company tag #10817, rarity 3, $45.00. (Collection of Richard Weinstein)

Plate 314. Swan on the Lake, ca. 1929, Nuart, gray metal, 5", shopmark, rarity 5*, $135.00.

Plate 315. Bird Takes a Bow, ca. 1925, bronze, 7½", rarity 5, $400.00. (Collection of Sue Benoliel)

Plate 316. Flapping Flamingoes, ca. 1930, Jennings Brothers, gray metal, 6½", shopmark #3024, rarity 4, $125.00.

Plate 317. Flamingoes, 1948, Everstyle (piece shown is unmarked, but identical piece with company markings has been seen), iron, 5¼", rarity 4, $125.00. (Design Patent #149282 for this piece was issued April 13, 1948, to Alexander Leva, New York, New York.)

Plate 318. Warbler, ca. 1930, Nuart, gray metal, shopmark, rarity 5*, $225.00.

Plate 319. Road Runner, ca. 1930, Ronson, gray metal, 4¾", company tag #16065, rarity 4, $150.00.

Plate 320. The Griffin, ca. 1932, K&O, gray metal, 5¾", shopmark, Yellowstone Park, Holz, rarity 5*, $200.00.

Plate 321. Take off, ca. 1925, Littco, iron, 7", rarity 4, $110.00.

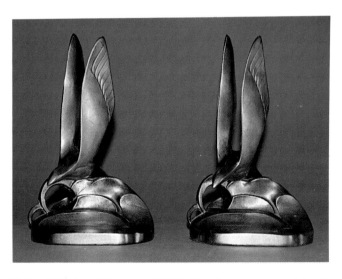

Plate 322. Perky Pheasant, ca. 1932, gray metal on marble base (most often seen on polished stone base), 6¾", rarity 4, $110.00.

Plate 323. Sea Bird, ca. 1934, Frankart, gray metal, 8", shopmark, rarity 5*, $210.00.

Plate 324. Pouter Pigeon, ca. 1928, gray metal, 6",
rarity 5, $75.00.

Plate 325. Indiana Pigeon, ca. 1940, Indiana Glass,
5½", rarity 3, $75.00.

Plate 325A. Opalescent finish, rarity 3, $70.00.

Plate 325B. Amber bird with frosted base, rarity 5*,
$150.00. (Collection of Michael Horseman)

Plate 326. Crane, ca. 1946, Dodge, gray metal, 6¾", rarity 4,
$75.00.

Plate 327. Silver Peacock, ca. 1914, Heintz Art
Metal, bronze with silver overlay, shopmark, 5", rarity 5, $175.00 – 400.00. (Collection of David Surgan)

Plate 328. Parrot and Perch, ca. 1934, Frankart, gray metal, 6¾", shopmark, rarity 5, $250.00.

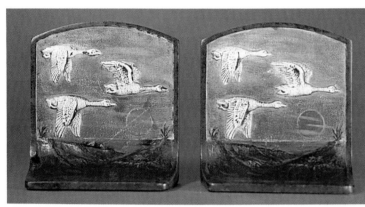

Plate 329. Flying Geese, ca. 1928, Judd, iron, 5½", #9688, rarity 5*, $165.00.

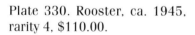

Plate 330. Rooster, ca. 1945, rarity 4, $110.00.

Plate 331. Silver Cormorant, ca. 1930, gray metal, 4¼", rarity 5*, $150.00. (Collection of Sue Benoliel)

Plate 332. Iron Ducks, ca. 1928, Littco, iron, 5', rarity 4, $125.00.

Plate 333. Sideglancing Rook, 1945, Rookwood, pottery, 6", shopmark #2274, rarity 5*, $600.00.

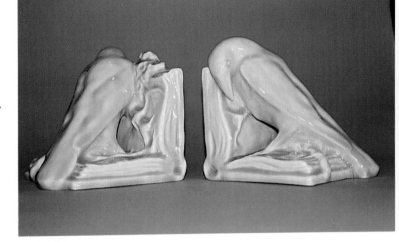

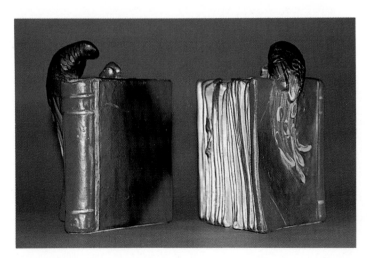

Plate 334. Parrot on Book, ca. 1928, K&O, gray metal, 6", shopmark, rarity 4, $125.00.

Plate 335. Kingfisher, ca. 1928, bronze in marble enclosure, 5¾", rarity 5*, $195.00.

Plate 336. Heron, ca. 1925, iron, 7½", rarity 5*, $175.00.

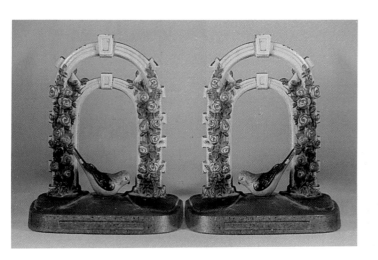

Plate 337. Flowered Bird, ca. 1925, iron, 6½", #1269, rarity 5*, $275.00.

Plate 338. Perched Parrot, ca. 1914, Heintz Art Metal, bronze with French gray bronze patina, 5½" shopmark, rarity 5, $175.00 – 400.00. (Collection of David Surgan)

Plate 339. Rooks, ca. 1940, Rookwood, 5¼", shopmark, IXIII 2275, designer initials of Wm. McDonald, rarity 5, $400.00. (Collection of Sue Benoliel)

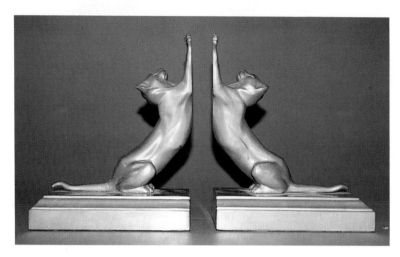

Plate 340. Cat, ca. 1932, pewter, 7", rarity 5, $175.00.

Plate 341. Geometric Cat, ca. 1935, gray metal, 8", rarity 3, $95.00.

Plate 342. Tiger and Snake, 1928, Connecticut Foundry, iron, 5", shopmark, Tiger and Snake, 1928, $65.00.

Plate 343. Rookwood Panther, ca. 1940, Rookwood, 5¼", shopmark, XLVI 2564, initials of designer, William P. McDonald, rarity 5, $450.00. (Collection of Sue Benoliel)

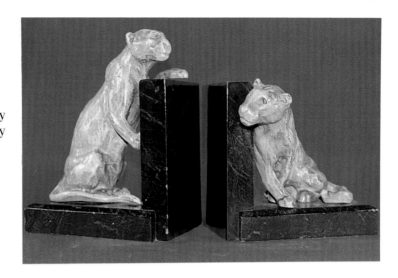

Plate 344. Panther Pair, ca. 1925, Ronson, gray metal on marbelized metal base, approx. 10", rarity 5*, $350.00. (Collection of Richard Weinstein)

Plate 345. Glass Tiger, ca. 1940, New Martinsville, 6½", rarity 5, $325.00. (Collection of Michael Horseman)

Plate 346. Facing the Lion, ca. 1928, Judd, iron, 4½", #9672, rarity 4, $125.00. (Courtesy Jay Mendlovitz)

Plate 347. African King, ca. 1925, attr. Littco, iron, 4¼", rarity 3, $85.00.

Plate 348. Cougars, ca. 1925, Armor Bronze, bronze clad, 5½", S. Morani, company tag, rarity 5, $175.00.

Plate 349. Lion of Lucerne (JB), ca. 1925, Jennings Brothers, gray metal, shopmark, #1258, 6", rarity 4, $125.00.

Plate 350. Lion of Lucerne, ca. 1920, Judd, iron (solid cast), approx. 5", rarity 5*, $175.00. (Courtesy of Rick Kushon, Etna Antiques, Etna, PA.)

Plate 351. Catwalk, ca. 1970, aluminum, approx. 3½", rarity 5, $25.00.

Plate 352. King of the Beasts, ca. 1934, K&O, gray metal, 5¾", shopmark, rarity 4, $90.00.

Plate 353. His Majesty, ca. 1925, attr. Judd, iron, 5¼", rarity 5*, $225.00.

Plate 354. King Tut's Meow, ca. 1930, gray metal, approx. 3½", rarity 5, $95.00. (Courtesy of Richard Weinstein)

Plate 355. Roar of the Tiger, ca.1925, Ronson, gray metal, 7½", company tag #8172, rarity 4, $175.00. (Collection of Richard Weinstein)

Plate 356. Two Lions, ca. 1926, iron, 4", rarity 3, $50.00.

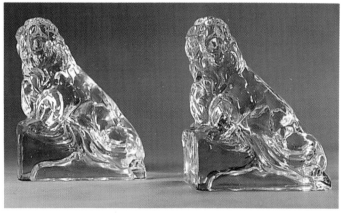

Plate 357. Glass Lion, ca. 1940, Cambridge Glass, 6", rarity 5, $200.00. (Collection of Michael Horseman)

Plate 358. Big Cat, ca. 1925, Moffatt, iron, 5½",
Moffatt, rarity 3, $75.00. (Piece shows Moffatt
shopmark, to date the only piece seen bearing
this mark.)

Plate 358A. Close-up of the insignia on the base of
Plate 358. It appears that the original insignia was a
stylized M, which subsequently evolved into the "bell"
seen on the base of all later pieces.

Plate 359. Close-up of the evolved "bell" emblem on later
Judd pieces. There is some likelihood that another company
took over the castings of Moffatt; since Judd did not have the
initial M, the emblem was modified. Identically cast pieces
appear in the catalogs of several companies, including Littco.

Plate 360. Amber Lion, 1978, Imperial Glass
Company, 6", rarity 4, $125.00. (Collection of
Michael Horseman)

CANINES

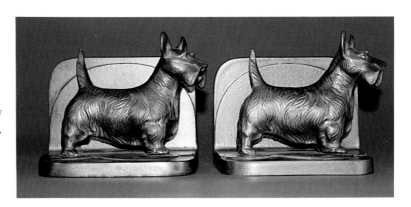

Plate 361. Scottie, ca. 1934, Frankart, gray metal, 4", marked Frankart, pat. appl. for, rarity 4, $125.00.

Plate 362. Dog, ca. 1925, Littco, iron, 4½", company tag, rarity 4, $125.00.

Plate 362A. Shopmark, Littco.

Plate 363. Scottie on Fence, ca. 1928, bronze, 6", rarity 5, $175.00.

Plate 364. All Ears, 1932, McClelland Barclay, gray metal, 6", signature, 1932, rarity 4, $175.00.

Plate 365. Hubley Scottie, ca. 1925, Hubley, iron, 5", rarity 3, $50.00. (Collection of Sue Benoliel)

Plate 366. Silver Scotties, ca. 1929, Jennings Brothers, gray metal, 5¼", shopmark, rarity 5, $125.00.

Plate 367. Auburn Scottie, ca. 1927, gray metal, 4¾", rarity 5, $100.00.

Plate 369. Scottish Terrier, 1929, Connecticut Foundry, iron, shopmark, scottish terrier, 1929, rarity 3, $50.00.

Plate 368. Scottie Pair, ca. 1934, Nuart, gray metal, 5", shopmark, rarity 2, $35.00.

Plate 371. Head Dog, ca. 1928, Frankart, gray metal, 6", Frankart, pat. appl. for, rarity 5, $175.00.

Plate 370. Scot, ca. 1929, gray metal, 7½", rarity 2, $40.00.

Plate 372. Retro Scottie, ca. 1930, Frankart, gray metal, 4½", shopmark, rarity 5, $125.00. Collection of Michael Horseman.

Plate 373. Glass Scottie, ca. 1940, Cambridge Glass, 6½", rarity 4, $125.00. (Collection of Michael Horseman)

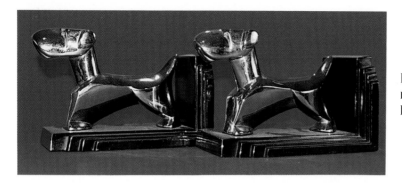

Plate 374. Chrome Scottie, ca. 1930, Ronson, gray metal, 5½", rarity 5*, $325.00. (Collection of Richard Weinstein)

Plate 375. Squatty Scottie, ca. 1940, approx. 5", rarity 3, $75.00.

Plate 376. Shepherd, ca. 1925, Bradley and Hubbard, iron, approx. 6", shopmark, rarity 5, $150.00.

Plate 377. Guarding the Flock, ca. 1925, X-1, gray metal, 5½", #610, rarity 5*, $195.00.

Plate 378. Nuart Shepherds, ca. 1930, Nuart, gray metal, 7", shopmark, rarity 3, $90.00. (Collection of Sue Benoliel)

Plate 379. Graceful Dane, ca. 1920, bronze, 6½", Austria, rarity 5*, $600.00. (Collection of Sue Benoliel)

Plate 380. On Alert, ca. 1930, brass, 6¼", rarity 4, $110.00.

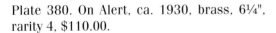

Plate 381. German Shepherd, ca. 1928, iron, 4¾", rarity 3, $45.00.

Plate 382. Paired Wolfhounds, ca. 1930, Ronson, approx. 4½", rarity 5, $110.00.

Plate 383. Hubley Shepherd, ca. 1925, Hubley, iron, 5", rarity 4, $150.00. (Collection of Sue Benoliel)

Plate 384. Police Dogs, ca. 1925, Jennings Brothers, gray metal, 5½", shopmark, #1922, rarity 5, $225.00.

Plate 385. Prancing Greyhound, ca. 1930, Ronson, gray metal, 6", rarity 5*, $325.00. (Collection of Richard Weinstein)

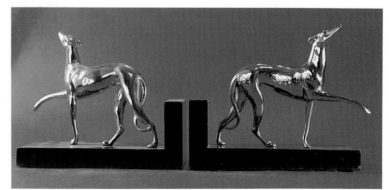

Plate 386. Leaping Greyhounds, ca. 1930, Ronson, gray metal, 5½", company tag #12314, rarity 5, $195.00. (Collection of Richard Weinstein)

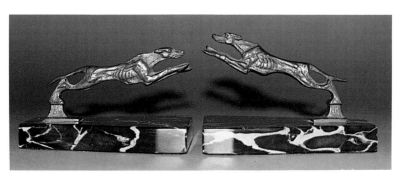

Plate 387. Leaping Greyhounds, ca. 1928, bronze on marble base, 3", rarity 5*, $175.00.

Plate 388. Wolfhound, ca. 1940, New Martinsville, 7", rarity 4, $200.00. (Collection of Michael Horseman)

Plate 389. Wire Terrier, 1929, Connecticut Foundry, iron, 5¾", Wire Terrier, 1929, rarity 3, $65.00.

Plate 390. Wirehaired Fox Terrier, ca. 1925, brass, 5", English registry mark, rarity 5*, $95.00. (Collection of Sue Benoliel)

Plate 391. Man's Best Friend, 1932, Ronson, 5", Ronson 1932 Newark, rarity 4, $105.00.

Plate 392. Pal, 1930, Connecticut Foundry, iron, 6½", PAL 1930, rarity 5*, $110.00.

Plate 393. Frisky Airedales, ca. 1925, Ronson, gray metal, 4¼", company tag #14473, rarity 5, $110.00.

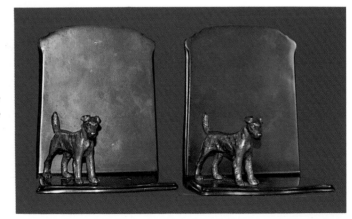

Plate 394. Beagle Dogs, ca. 1940, Rookwood, 6", shopmark XXIX, rarity 5, $400.00. (Collection of Sue Benoliel)

Plate 395. Tiperari Dog, ca. 1930, Ronson, gray metal, 6", company tag #1073, rarity 5, $175.00. (Collection of Richard Weinstein)

Plate 396. Fido, ca. 1925, Bronzart, gray metal, shopmark, (figure partially obscures shopmark on base, found under left rear foot), 6½", rarity 4, $165.00.

Plate 397. Orphans, ca. 1923, iron, 4½", #272, rarity 4, $100.00.

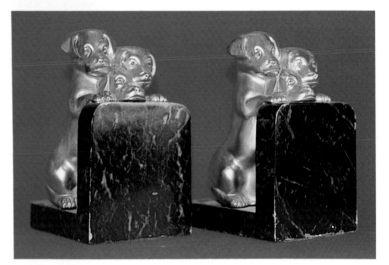

Plate 398. Perky Puppies, ca. 1928, Armor Bronze, bronze clad, approx. 4", shopmark, rarity 4. $95.00.

Plate 399. Puppy Triplets, ca. 1925, Ronson, gray metal on marbleized metal base, 6", company tag #14035, rarity 4, $165.00. (Collection of Richard Weinstein)

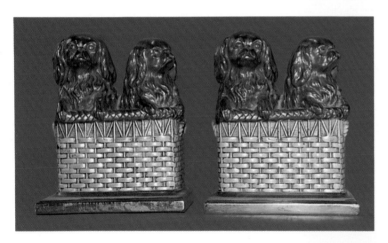

Plate 400. Pekingese Pups, ca. 1930, Ronson, gray metal, 5¼", company tag #16601, rarity 5, $150.00. (Collection of Richard Weinstein)

Plate 401. Pekingese Peek-a-boo, ca. 1925, Ronson, gray metal on marbleized gray metal base, company tag, 5½", rarity 5, $200.00. (Collection of Richard Weinstein)

Plate 402. Pert Pups, ca. 1925, Hubley, iron, approx 5", rarity 5 (polychrome), 4 other finishes, $175.00 (polychrome), $125.00 (other finishes). (Collection of Sue Benoliel)

Plate 403. Cocker Spaniel, ca. 1934, Frankart, gray metal, 6¼", shopmark, rarity 4, $150.00.

Plate 404. Spunky Spaniel, ca. 1930, gray metal, 5", rarity 4, $100.00. (Collection of Sue Benoliel)

Plate 405. Latticework and Dog, 1930, C Company, iron, 6", C Co., 1930 copyright, rarity 5, $200.00.

Plate 406. Half-breed, ca. 1920, iron, 6", rarity 5*, $175.00.

Plate 407. Plains Wolf, 1923, Ronson, gray metal, 4¼", LV, Aronson, 1923, rarity 4, $125.00. (Collection of Richard Weinstein)

Plate 408. Great Dane, ca. 1928, J.F. Co., gray metal, 7¾", shopmark, rarity 4, $125.00.

Plate 409. Pensive Hound, ca. 1930, Ronson, gray metal, 3¼", company tag #16031, rarity 3, $95.00. (Collection of Richard Weinstein)

Plate 410. Boxer, ca. 1930, gray metal, 6¼", rarity 5, $175.00.

Plate 411. Mastiff, ca. 1926, Bradley and Hubbard, iron, 5¼", shopmark, rarity 4, $165.00.

Plate 412. Seated Russian Wolfhound, ca. 1925, iron, 6½", England, rarity 5*, $150.00. (Collection of Sue Benoliel)

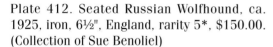

Plate 413. Retriever Dog, 1920 – 1930, bronze, English registry mark #694237, rarity 5*, $275.00. (Collection of Sue Benoliel)

Plate 414. Hunting Dog, ca. 1925, attr. Hubley, bronze 4½", rarity 3, $125.00. (Courtesy Jay Mendlovitz)

Plate 415. Setter Dog, 1922, Ronson, gray metal, 3¼", LVA 1922, rarity 5, $125.00. (Collection of Richard Weinstein)

Plate 416. Hound and Bird, ca. 1934, Frankart, gray metal, 5", Frankart, Inc., pat. appl. for, rarity 4, $210.00.

Plate 417. Hound, ca. 1930, Ronson, gray metal, 5¾", rarity 4, $150.00.

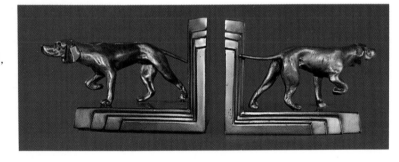

Plate 418. Dog at the Fence, ca. 1930, Frankart, gray metal, 6", shopmark, rarity 5*, $250.00.

Plate 419. Setters, ca. 1925, Littco, iron, 5",
rarity 4, $115.00.

Plate 420. Pointers, ca. 1925, Hubley, iron, 4¼",
rarity 4 (polychrome), 3 (other finishes), $95.00
(polychrome, $75.00 (other finishes). (Collection of
Sue Benoliel)

Plate 421. The Hunter and His Dog, ca. 1925, Hubley, iron, 6¼", #423, rarity 5, $450.00. (Collection
of Sue Benoliel)

Plate 422. Sailor Boy and Dog, ca. 1934, Frankart,
gray metal, 6¾", shopmark, rarity 4, $185.00.

Plate 423. Companions, ca. 1929, WB, gray metal, 7",
shopmark, rarity 5*, $195.00.

Plate 424. Ibex Leap, ca. 1920, Littco, iron, 5", rarity 3, $125.00.

Plate 425. Goat, ca. 1928, Jennings Brothers, gray metal, 5", shopmark, rarity 5*, $110.00.

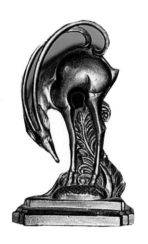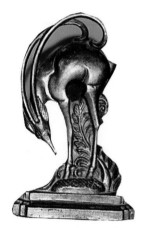

Plate 427. Ibex Couple, ca. 1925, Hubley, iron, 5", #417, rarity 4, $175.00. (Collection of Sue Benoliel)

Plate 426. Longhorn Gazelle, 1932, Crescent Metal Works, gray metal, 7¼", shopmark, 1932, rarity 4, $160.00.

Plate 429. Glass Gazelle, ca. 1940, New Martinsville, 8¼", rarity 4, $125.00. (Collection of Michael Horseman)

Plate 428. Rams, 1974, SCC, gray metal, 7", SCC, rarity 2, $35.00.

Plate 430. Feeding Gazelle, ca. 1930, attr. Ronson, gray metal, 5", rarity 4, $125.00.

Plate 431. Deco Doe, ca. 1929, gray metal on iron base, 6", rarity 5, $125.00.

Plate 432. Leaping Gazelle, ca. 1930, Crescent Metal Works, gray metal, 7¼", shopmark, rarity 3, $85.00.

Plate 433. Doe, ca. 1934, Frankart, gray metal, 5¼", shopmark, rarity 3, $125.00.

Plate 434. Gazelle, ca. 1925, Hubley, iron, rarity 4, $125.00.

Plate 435. Moose Revenge, ca. 1930, glass, approx. 7", rarity 5*, $175.00.

Plate 436. Stag, 1925 (figure is patented June 30, 1925, #67, 706 Design Patent, by Jack Katz of New York, NY), X-1, gray metal, #508, rarity 5, $275.00.

ELEPHANTS

Plate 437. Elephant Heads, ca. 1928, Jennings Brothers, gray metal, 7", shopmark, #1531, rarity 5, $185.00. (Collection of Sue Benoliel)

Plate 438. Trumpeting Elephants, ca. 1925, Ronson, gray metal with celluloid tusks, 4¼", company tag #16333, rarity 5, $125.00. (Collection of Richard Weinstein)

Plate 439. Elephant Heads, 1922, Ronson, gray metal, 4", LV Aronson 1922, rarity 5, $110.00. (Collection of Richard Weinstein)

Plate 440. Like Father, Like Son, ca. 1925, gray metal on marble base, 7", rarity 4, $125.00.

Plate 441. Working for Peanuts, ca. 1925, iron, 4½", rarity 3, $85.00. (Collection of Sue Benoliel)

Plate 442. We're Home, Dad, ca. 1925, attr. JB Hirsch, gray metal with celluloid tusks, on polished stone base, 6", rarity 5, $175.00.

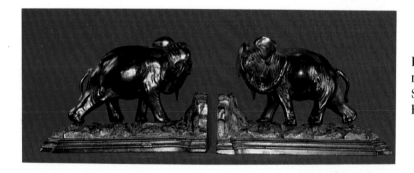

Plate 443. Trunk Aside, ca. 1925, Ronson, gray metal, 5", company tag #8173, rarity 3, $150.00, polychrome $165.00. (Collection of Richard Weinstein)

Plate 444. Elephant Terrain, ca. 1930, Ronson, gray metal 6⅛", company tag #14159, rarity 3, $95.00. (Collection of Richard Weinstein)

Plate 445. Best Foot Forward, ca. 1930, attr. JB Hirsch, cast gray metal, 5", rarity 4, $125.00.

Plate 446. Trouble Underfoot, ca. 1926, Littco, iron, 4¼", rarity 4, $110.00.

Plate 447. Climbing Elephant, 1922, Ronson, gray metal, 5¼", Company tag #10550, rarity 4, $125.00. (Collection of Richard Weinstein)

Plate 448. Elephant, 1930, Connecticut Foundry, iron, 5¾", shopmark, Elephant copyright 1930, rarity 3, $75.00.

Plate 449. Elephant at Tree, ca. 1925, Judd Co., iron, 4½", shopmark, rarity 4, $150.00.

Plate 450. Elephant on Library, ca. 1918, Ronson, gray metal, 4", rarity 4, $110.00.

Plate 451. Pedestalized Elephant, ca. 1924, Ronson, gray metal, 4¼", company tag #11249, rarity 5, $150.00. (Collection of Richard Weinstein)

Plate 452. Begging for Peanuts, ca. 1930, Ronson, gray metal, 4¼", company tag #14018, rarity 4, $150.00. (Collection of Richard Weinstein)

Plate 453. Elephant Country, 1923, Ronson, gray metal, 4", LV Aronson, 1923, rarity 5, $125.00.

Plate 454. Howdah Elephant, 1923, Ronson, gray metal, 4½", LV Aronson, 1923, rarity 3, $125.00 (polychrome), $110.00 (other finishes).

Plate 455. Geometric Elephant, 1928, Andersen-Starr, gray metal, 5½", A-S, rarity 5, $275.00. (This piece is design patented #76,113 to Alf B Andersen and Starr of NY, NY, August 21, 1928.)

Plate 456. African Elephant, ca. 1920, iron, 5½", rarity 4, $125.00.

Plate 457. Elephant Challenge, ca. 1926, Ronson, gray metal, 6", company tag #195M, rarity 3, $175.00.

Plate 458. Ultra-modern Elephants, ca. 1933, Chase (designer: von Nessen), brass and plastic, 4¾", rarity 5, $550.00.

Plate 459. White Elephants, ca. 1930, gray metal, 4¾", rarity 3, $75.00.

Plate 460. Elephants' Run of the Library, ca. 1930, Jennings Brothers, 8½", shopmark (hardly visible, located on inner thigh), rarity 5*, $350.00.

Plate 461. Clearly An Elephant, ca. 1940, New Martinsville, 5½", rarity 4, $150.00. (Collection of Michael Horseman)

Plate 462. Leaping Horse, ca. 1934, Nuart, gray metal, 5¾", rarity 4, $85.00.

Plate 463. White Horses, ca. 1935, gray metal on iron base, 6¼", "White" emblem, rarity 3, $110.00.

Plate 464. Prancing Horses, ca. 1934, Frankart, gray metal, 5¾", shopmark, rarity 4, $125.00.

Plate 465. Horse on Arc, ca. 1947, Dodge, gray metal, 5½", rarity 3, $60.00.

Plate 466. Looking Back, ca. 1935, gray metal, 6½", Kraftware, rarity 4, $75.00. (Collection of Sue Benoliel)

Plate 467. Chase Horse, ca. 1935, Chase, bronze, 6¼", rarity 5, $600.00.

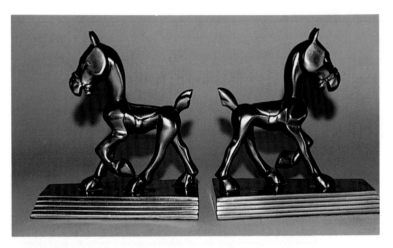

Plate 468A. Company tag, K&O.

Plate 468. Caricature Pony, ca. 1935, K&O, gray metal, 5½", shopmark, rarity 5*, $150.00.

Plate 469. Pony, ca. 1926, Littco, iron, 6", rarity 4, $110.00.

Plate 470. Miniature Horses, ca. 1930, Sellright Giftware Corporation, gray metal, 4¼", company tag, rarity 4, $85.00

Plate 471. Grazing Pony, ca. 1930, gray metal, 5¼", rarity 4, $110.00.

Plate 472. Burro, ca. 1925, Hubley, iron, 4", Made in USA, #492, rarity 5*, $150.00.

Plate 473. Thoroughbred Horse Head, ca. 1930, gray metal, 4⅛", company tag #16339, rarity 4, $95.00.

Plate 474. Chariot Horses, ca. 1934, Frankart, gray metal, 5", Frankart Inc. pat. appl. for, rarity 4, $150.00.

Plate 475. Horse Head, ca. 1935, bronze, 5", rarity 5*, $175.00.

Plate 476. Grand Pegasus, ca. 1925, gray metal on polished stone base, 7¾", rarity 5*, $275.00.

Plate 477. Horse Family, ca. 1930, Judd, iron, 5¼", shopmark #09855, rarity 5, $95.00.

Plate 478. Drucklieb Horses, ca. 1926, H Co., gray metal, 5¾", artist signature, (Jeanne L. Drucklieb copyright), H, rarity 5*, $165.00. (Collection of Sue Benoliel)

Plate 479. Ye Olde Coaching Days, ca. 1924, Jennings Brothers, gray metal, 4¼", shopmark #2385, rarity 3, $65.00.

Plate 480. Man-O-War, ca. 1924, Z-R, iron, 6", rarity 5, $160.00.

Plate 481. Mythic Chariot, 1930, Hoyt Metal Company, bronze, A Souvenir Marking the Opening of our New Brass Foundry, Hoyt Metal Co. of Canada, LTD, June 23, 1930, G.F. Allen, L.P. Francis, V.P. Bingham, 4½" rarity 5*, $175.00.

Plate 482. Twin Horses, ca. 1930, Ronson, gray metal, 3½", company tag #16417, rarity 4, $100.00. (Collection of Richard Weinstein)

Plate 483. Horse in Horseshoe, ca. 1930, Ronson gray metal, 4⅝", company tag #16513, rarity 4, $95.00. (Collection of Richard Weinstein)

Plate 484. Horse on the Loose, ca. 1930, Jennings Brothers, gray metal, 6½", shopmark, rarity 5, $195.00. (Courtesy Jay Mendlovitz)

Plate 485. Listening to the Wind, ca. 1930, Armor Bronze, bronze clad, 6¼", shopmark, rarity 5, $95.00.

Plate 486. Prancers, ca. 1932, K&O gray metal, 10", rarity 5*, $125.00.

Plate 487. Riderless Horse, ca. 1930, bronze, 4¾", rarity (bronze) 5, (iron) 3, $110.00 (bronze), $45.00 (iron).

Plate 488. Prancing Pegasus, ca. 1928, Judd, iron, approx. 6", shopmark, rarity 4, $85.00.

Plate 489. Desert Rider, ca. 1929, bronze, 5¼", rarity 5*, $210.00.

Plate 490. Roman Horseman, ca. 1928, Littco, iron, 6", rarity 3, $50.00.

Plate 491. Lancelette, ca. 1929, attr. JB Hirsch, gray metal with celluloid face, on polished stone base, 6", rarity 5, $275.00.

Plate 492. Drug Trip, ca. 1934, Nuart, gray metal, shopmark, rarity 5, $250.00.

Plate 493. Cowboy and Broncho, 1930, Connecticut Foundry, iron, 6", shopmark, "Cowboy and Broncho," 1930, #923, rarity 5*, $125.00.

Plate 494. Bronco Rider, ca. 1947, Dodge, gray metal, 5", rarity 4, $75.00.

Plate 495. Ride 'em Cowboy, ca. 1932, Armor Bronze, bronze clad, 6¾", signed Paul Hertzel, rarity 5, $200.00. (Collection of Sue Benoliel)

Plate 496. Chariot Rounding the Bend, ca. 1930, iron, 6¼", #695, rarity 4, $75.00 (also seen in bronze, rarity 5, $135.00).

Plate 497. Jumper, ca. 1930, Jennings Brothers, gray metal, rarity 5, $145.00. (This piece has been altered, although skillfully done, and I did not detect it at the time of purchase. Subsequently, seeing an intact piece indicates a short tail was present. Likely, the tail was damaged on one piece, requiring some "adjustment" to make a suitable pair, hence the new tail.)

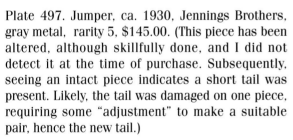

Plate 498. Rose Jockey, ca. 1932, attr. JB Hirsch, gray metal on polished stone base, 5", rarity 5, $135.00.

Plate 499. Photo Finish, ca. 1928, Jennings Brothers, gray metal, shopmark #809, 4¼", rarity 5, $275.00.

Plate 500. Horeserace, ca. 1934, Nuart, gray metal, 4¼", company shopmark, rarity 5*, $250.00.

Plate 501. Rough Rider, ca. 1925, iron, 5½", rarity 4, $100.00. (Collection of Sue Benoliel)

Plate 502. Polo Player, ca. 1928, Littco, iron, 5½", rarity 4, $85.00.

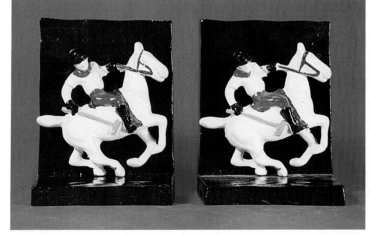

Plate 503. Stagecoach, ca. 1925, Hubley, iron, 4", #379, rarity 4, $150.00. (Collection of Sue Benoliel)

Plate 504. Empty Coach, 1931, Champion, iron, 3¼", shopmark, Geneva, 1931, rarity 3, $35.00.

Plate 505. Head Up Horse, ca. 1940, New Martinsville, 8", rarity 5, $190.00.

Plate 506. Over the Top, 1947, Haley, 7½", rarity 4, $110.00.

Plate 507. New Martinsville Horse, ca. 1940, New Martinsville Glass Company, 7½", rarity 4, $150.00. (Collection of Michael Horseman)

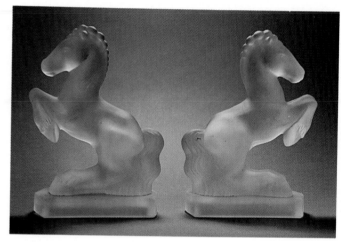

Plate 508. Smith Horse, ca. 1925, 8", rarity 4, $100.00.

Plate 509. Smith Horse, ca. 1925, 8", rarity 3, $75.00.

Plate 510. Smith Horse, different glass color, rarity 5, $150.00.

Plate 511. Jumping Horse, ca. 1940, 8", rarity 4, $100.00.

Plate 512. Rearing Horse, 1980, Heisey re-issue, rarity 5*, $400.00.

Plate 513. Lady Godiva, ca. 1940, Haley, 6", rarity 4, $135.00.

Plate 514. Up to My Neck, ca. 1940, approx. 5", rarity 4, $75.00.

Plate 515. Federal Horse, ca. 1940, Federal Glass, 5½", rarity 1, $10.00. (Collection of Michael Horseman)

Plate 515A. Same as Plate 515, different color, rarity 2, $15.00.

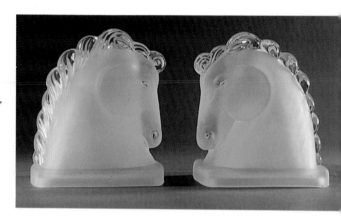

Plate 516. Heisey Horse Head, 1937 – 1955, Heisey, 6½", rarity 4, $240.00.

Plate 516A. Same as Plate 516, frosted, rarity 4, $200.00.

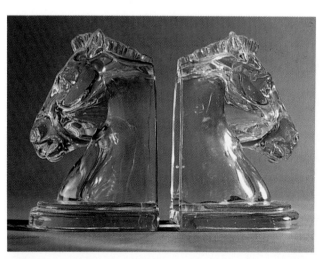

Plate 517. Indiana Horse Head, ca. 1940, Indiana Glass, 6", rarity 3, $50.00.

MARINE LIFE

Plate 518. Kissing Fish, ca. 1925, Littco, iron, 5", rarity 3, $95.00. (Collection of Sue Benoliel)

Plate 519. Angelfish, ca. 1930, attr. JB Hirsch, gray metal on polished stone base, 6", rarity 3, $120.00.

Plate 520. No Halo, ca. 1940, approx. 6½", rarity 4, $125.00.

Plate 521. Glass Angelfish, ca. 1940, American Glass
Company, 8¼", rarity 4, $135.00.

Plate 522. Goldfish, 1992, Rookwood, pottery,
4½", shopmark, rarity 4, $85.00.

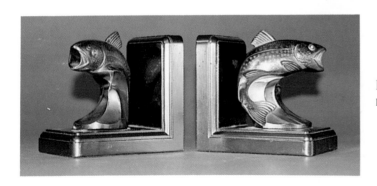

Plate 523. Trout, ca. 1965, PM Craftsman, gray
metal, 4", PMC, rarity 3, $50.00.

Plate 524. Trout, ca. 1934, gray metal, 6½",
rarity 4, $125.00.

Plate 525. Sailfish, ca. 1965, PM Craftsman, gray metal, 8", shopmark, rarity 3, $65.00.

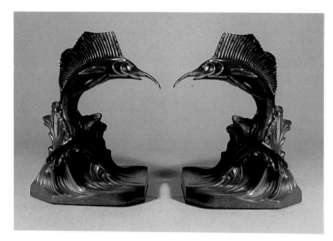

Plate 526. Sailfish and Wave, ca. 1928, Jennings Brothers, gray metal, 5", shopmark, #1258, rarity 4, $110.00.

Plate 527. Deco Marlin, ca. 1935, chrome and bronze, 3¼" rarity 5*, $225.00.

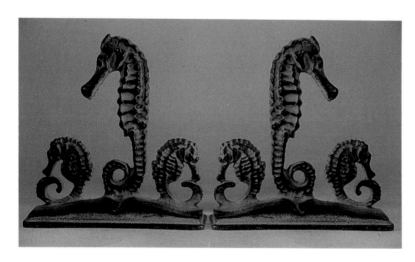

Plate 528. The Seahorse Family, ca. 1925, iron, 5¾", rarity 3, $75.00.

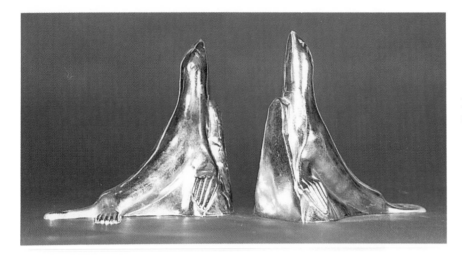

Plate 529. Deco Seal, ca. 1930, chrome, 6¼", rarity 5*, $175.00.

Plate 530. Barclay Seals, ca. 1935, McClelland Barclay, gray metal, 6", McClelland Barclay, rarity 4, $150.00.

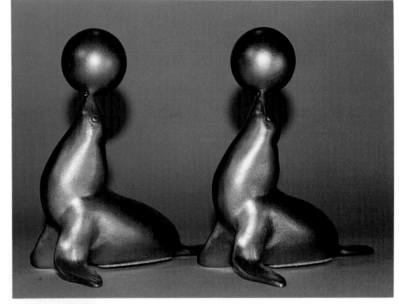

Plate 531. Sleek Seals, ca. 1930, Ronson, gray metal, 8", company tag #14661, rarity 5, $225.00. (Collection of Richard Weinstein)

Plate 532. Whale, ca. 1965, PM Craftsman, gray metal, 7½", company label, rarity 3, $50.00.

Plate 533. Mermaid, ca. 1930, gray metal, 6", rarity 5, $250.00.

Plate 534. Mermaids, ca. 1925, attr. JB Hirsch, gray metal on marble base, 5", rarity 5*, $275.00.

Those Who Go Down To The Sea In Ships

The 300th anniversary of the town of Gloucester, Massachusetts, was observed in 1923, and the community marked this event by designating a 65-person committee to seek an appropriate idea for a memorial to the fishermen of the community. A Mr. Walen submitted the winning entry, using his father as the model, and sculptor Leonard Craske was assigned to execute the piece. The final product was unveiled on August 23, 1925. The pose is of a helmsman with his eyes fixed on the sails as he brings his craft up as close as possible to avoid dangerous rocks. The base is of sea green granite quarried from the Bay View section of Gloucester. The sculpture is intended as a memorial to all Gloucester fishermen who lost their lives while fishing, and faces the outer harbor in Gloucester still today.

This sculpture is sometimes mistaken for "Man At The Wheel," a painting by Buhler, which became the logo for retail products of the Gorton Fisheries company, also of Gloucester, Massachusetts.

Bookends reproduced from the piece come in a variety of finishes, of which the most rare is antique silver. Recently, the piece has been produced by Philadelphia Metal Craftsman, of Lakeland, Florida, but the patina is distinctly different from that of the older pieces. This apparently was a very popular piece, seen as a lamp, ashtray, and other adaptations.

Plate 535. Those Who Go Down to the Sea In Ships, ca. 1980, attr. Philadelphia Metal Craftsman, rarity 5, $125.00.

Plate 535A. Same as Plate 535, different finish, rarity 5*, $225.00.

Plate 536. Those Who Go Down to the Sea in lamp form.

Plate 537. Weather-beaten Mariner, ca. 1930, Ronson, gray metal, 5¼", company tag #16368, rarity 5*, $165.00.

Plate 538. Steady at the Wheel, ca. 1925, iron, 5½", rarity 5*, $175.00.

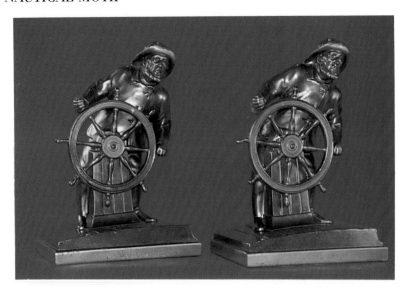

Plate 539. Weather-beaten Mariner, ca. 1930, Ronson, gray metal, 6", rarity 4, $150.00. (Collection of Richard Weinstein)

Plate 540. Anchor (Dodge), ca. 1947, attr. Dodge, gray metal, 5¾", rarity 3, $45.00.

Plate 541. Cape Cod Fisherman, 1928, Connecticut Foundry, iron, 5½", shopmark, Cape Cod Fisherman, 1928, rarity 3, $65.00.

Plate 542. Lighting the Way, ca. 1930, attr. JB Hirsch, gray metal with celluloid face, on polished stone base, 8", rarity 5, $225.00.

Plate 543. Lighting the Way-Anchored, attr. JB Hirsch, ca. 1930, gray metal with celluloid face, on polished stone base, 8", rarity 5, $225.00.

Plate 544. New Bedford Whaler, ca. 1930, Jennings Brothers, gray metal, 7", JB 3139: In Honor of the Whaleman Whose Skill Hardihood and Daring Brought Fame and Fortune to New Bedford and Made its Name Known In Every Seaport of the Globe, rarity 5, $350.00. (Re-issues by PMC show a much more polished finish, value $100.00.) Designed in 1913 by Bela Lyon Pratt, stands now in front of the New Bedford Library; inscription reads 'a dead whale or a stove boat.'

Plate 545. Lighthouse and Seagull, ca. 1928, bronze, Graham, rarity 5, $200.00. (Collection of Sue Benoliel)

Plate 546. Pilot Wheel, ca. 1940, Chase, polished brass with natural walnut and brown plastic, 6⅜", shopmark, rarity 4, $175.00.

Plate 547. Pilot Wheel, ca. 1930, Ronson, gray metal, 4¾", company tag #16572, rarity 4, $110.00. (Collection of Richard Weinstein)

Plate 548. Pilot Wheel and Anchor, ca. 1930, Ronson gray metal, 4¾", company tag #16444, rarity 5, $150.00. (Collection of Richard Weinstein)

Plate 549. Anchors (Chase), ca. 1935, Chase, Inc., brass, 6¼", shopmark, rarity 3, $100.00.

Plate 549A. Same As Plate 549, different finish.

Plate 550. Bronze Anchor, ca. 1930, bronze, 5", rarity 5*, $295.00.

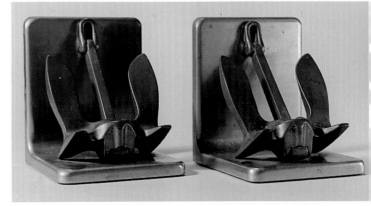

Plate 551. Frigate Constitution, ca. 1920, Gorham Bronze, Hugo Carlborg, Sc., 5¾", rarity 5*, $425.00.

Plate 552. Warship, ca. 1927, iron, rarity 2, $30.00.

Plate 553. Galleon Voyage, ca. 1925, Ronson, gray metal, approx. 5", rarity 4, $90.00.

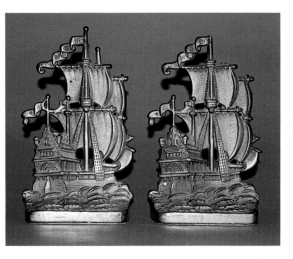

Plate 554. Two Flags, 1928, Seville Studios, iron, 9", shopmark, rarity 4, $85.00.

Plate 555. Treasure Ship, ca. 1927, Armor Bronze, bronze clad, 7½", Vanderogen, 1560, rarity 4, $110.00.

Plate 556. Ride the Waves, ca. 1925, AM Greenblatt Studios, brass, 5½", rarity 4, $120.00.

Plate 557. Occupied Japan Galleon, ca. 1946, gray metal, 6¾", Made in Occupied Japan, CPO, rarity 4, $75.00.

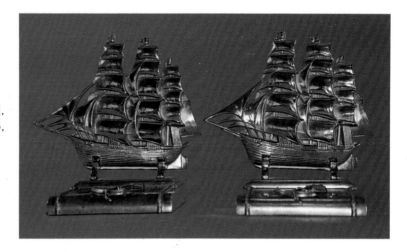

Plate 558. Full-rigger, 1940, Ronson, gray metal, 5¼", 1940 AMW Inc., Newark NJ USA, rarity 5, $110.00. (Collection of Richard Weinstein)

Plate 559. Spanish Galleon, ca. 1925, Ronson, gray metal, 4½", rarity 3, $50.00.

Plate 560. Full Sails, 1930, Connecticut Foundry, iron, 4½", shopmark, 1930, #901, rarity 2, $20.00.

Plate 561. Ocean Voyage, ca. 1927, Bradley and Hubbard, iron, 5½", shopmark, rarity 3, $70.00.

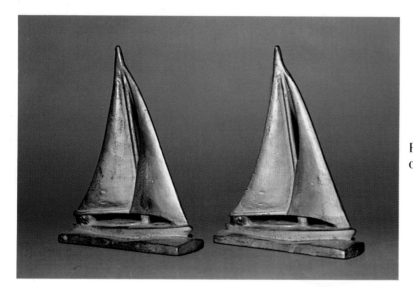

Plate 562. Sailboat, ca. 1929, Littco, iron, 7½", company tag, rarity 4, $100.00.

Plate 563. Speedboat, ca. 1934, Jennings Brothers, gray metal, 3½", shopmark, rarity 5, $200.00.

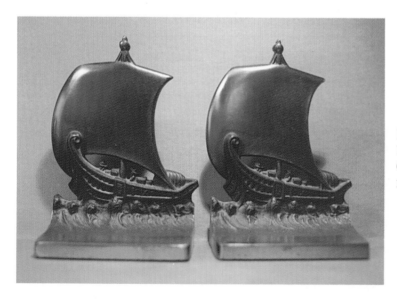

Plate 564. Viking Ship, ca. 1928, Bradley and Hubbard, iron (also seen in solid bronze), shopmark, 6" (also comes as doorstop, substantially larger), rarity 4, $95.00. (Collection of Sue Benoliel)

EGYPTIAN MOTIF

Plate 565. Sphinx, ca. 1926, iron, 3¾", $20.00.

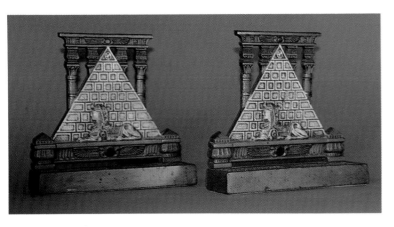

Plate 566. Guarding Pharoah, Judd, ca. 1926, iron, 6¼", #9743, rarity 5, $225.00.

Plate 567. Egyptian Tomb, ca. 1926, attr. Judd, iron, 6½", rarity 5, $160.00.

Plate 568. Egyptian Birds, ca. 1928, Judd, iron, approx. 4½", shopmark, rarity 5*, $115.00. (Courtesy Gail Salsky)

Plate 569. Egyptian Face, ca. 1930, bronze, approx. 6", rarity 5, $175.00.

Plate 570. Judd Sphinx, ca. 1925, attr. Judd, approx. 8", iron, rarity 5, $325.00.

Plate 571. Pharaoh, ca. 1926, Armor Bronze, 7", bronze clad, shopmark, signed L. Cudebrod, Sc., rarity 4, $175.00.

Plate 572. Nude on Sphinx, ca. 1925, attr. Armor Bronze, bronze clad, approx. 6", rarity 5, $175.00.

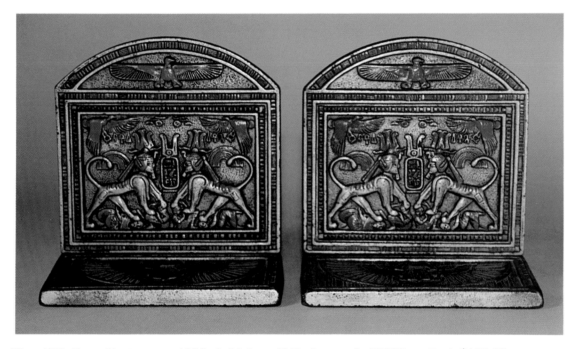

Plate 573. Egypt Fantasy, ca. 1926, Judd, iron, 5¼", shopmark, #9660, rarity 4, $125.00.

Plate 574. Egyptian Camel, 1928, Connecticut Foundry, iron, 6", shopmark, Egyptian Camel, 1928, rarity 4, $95.00.

Plate 575. Foo Dogs, ca. 1920, iron, 5", rarity 5, $175.00.

Plate 576. Buddha, 1922, Ronson, gray metal, 6¼", LV Aronson, 1922, company tag #8505, rarity 5, $135.00. (Collection of Richard Weinstein)

Plate 576A. Another Ronson Buddha, 1922 4", marked LVA, rarity 5, $95.00.

Plate 577. Oriental Meditation, ca. 1930, Solid Bronze, bronze, 6", shopmark, rarity 5, $225.00.

Plate 578. Chinese Man, ca. 1933, attr. JB Hirsch, gray metal, 8¼", rarity 5, $150.00.

Plate 579. Tiffany Buddha, ca. 1930, Tiffany, bronze, 5¾", shopmark, rarity 4, $450.00. (Collection of Sue Benoliel)

Plate 580. Japanese Woman, ca. 1929, Jennings Brothers, gray metal, 8½", shopmark, #1808, rarity 4, $110.00.

Plate 581. Geisha, ca. 1925, Pompeian Bronze, gray metal, 4¾", Geisha, PB Inc., rarity 3, $90.00.

Plate 582. Asian Home, ca. 1950, 4", brass, rarity 4, $95.00.

Plate 583. Siam Couple, ca. 1926, iron, 4¾", rarity 3, $65.00.

Plate 583A. Same as Plate 583 except Solid Bronze. Note the difference in detail. rarity 4, $150.00.

Plate 584. The Tutor, ca. 1925, Pompeian Bronze, gray metal, 4¼", PB & Co, The Tutor, rarity 5*, $200.00.

Plate 585. Lyre, ca. 1965, PM Craftsman, gray metal, 6", PMC, rarity 2, $45.00.

Plate 586. Lady Jester, ca. 1929, X-1, gray metal, 7¼", #66, rarity 5* (polychrome), 5 (other finishes), $375.00 (polychrome), $325.00 (other finishes).

Plate 586A. Same as Plate 586, showing reverse markings.

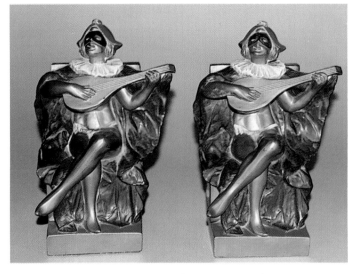

Plate 586B. Same as Plate 586, polychrome finish.

Plate 587. Angelic Harpist, ca. 1928, attr. Hirsch, gray metal on polished stone base, 6½", rarity 5*, $295.00.

Plate 588. Pierrot Plays, ca. 1925, gray metal, rarity 5, $175.00. Similar to Plate 589.

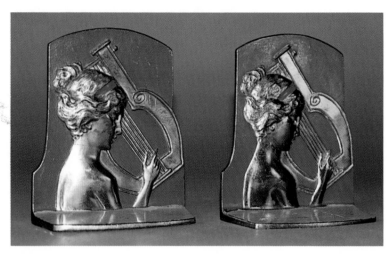

Plate 589. Minstrel Clown, ca. 1929, K&O, gray metal on marble base, 5¼", rarity 4, $175.00.

Plate 590. Celeste, ca. 1925, Ronson, gray metal, 5", rarity 5*, $225.00.

Plate 591. Roman Cellist, 1921, (copyright #63561 Issued to "Peter Maneredi, of Italy, domiciled in the US," August 31, 1921), Pompeian Bronze, 6½", shopmark, bronze clad, rarity 4, $135.00.

Plate 592. Serenade, ca. 1929, iron, 4¼", rarity 5* $175.00.

Plate 593. The Wanderer, 1930, Connecticut Foundry, iron, The Wanderer, 1930, shopmark, 5¾", rarity 5, $125.00.

Plate 594. King's Minstrel, ca. 1925, attr. JB Hirsch gray metal with celluloid face, on marble base, 7¾" rarity 5*, $350.00.

Plate 595. Serenade Tonight, ca. 1925, Hubley, iron, 5½", #233, rarity 5* (polychrome), 4 (bronze finish), $275.00 (polychrome), $125.00 (other finishes).

Plate 595A. Same as Plate 595, bronze finish.

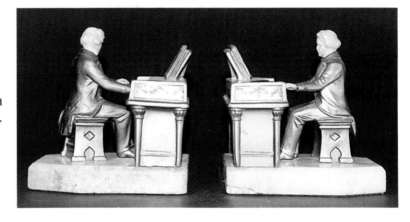

Plate 596. Beethoven, 1932, gray metal on marble base, 4½", JBH 1932, rarity 5, $250.00.

Plate 596A. Same as Plate 596, different finish.

Plate 597. Cellists, ca. 1932, JB Hirsch, gray meta with celluloid face, on polished stone base, 6½", JBH rarity 4, $200.00.

Plate 599. Glass Lyre, 1942 – 1944, Fostoria Glass, 7", rarity 4, $150.00. (Collection of Michael Horseman)

Plate 598. Cellists, ca. 1940, JB Hirsch, chalk on polished stone base, JBH, rarity 4, $135.00.

Rear view, Plate 600, showing JB Hirsch shopmark and Ruhl signature.

Plate 600. Classical Cellists, 1932, JB Hirsch, gray metal with celluloid faces, on polished stone base, 6½", rarity 4, $225.00.

NATURAL MOTIF

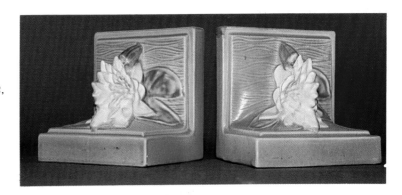

Plate 601. Roseville, ca. 1940, Roseville, ceramic, 5", rarity 3, $175.00.

Plate 602. Foxglove, ca. 1940, Roseville, 5", pottery, shopmark, rarity 5, $325.00.

Plate 603. Lily pad, ca. 1945, Dodge, gray metal, 4½", company tag, rarity 3, $65.00. (Collection of Sue Benoliel)

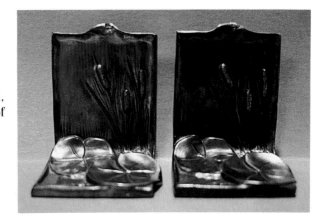

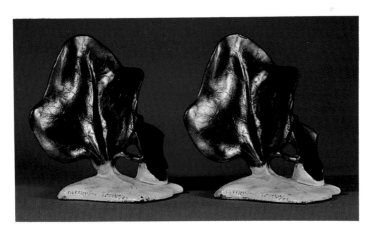

Plate 604. Autumn Leaves, ca. 1930, gray metal, 5¾", McClelland Barclay, rarity 5*, $275.00.

Plate 605. Maple Leaf, ca. 1965, PM Craftsman, gray metal, 6", PMC, 57D, rarity 3, $40.00.

Plate 606. Oak Leaf, ca. 1965, PM Craftsman, gray metal, 6½", shopmark, rarity 3, $45.00.

Plate 607. Dogwood, ca. 1965, PM Craftsman, gray metal, 5¼", shopmark, rarity 3, $40.00.

Plate 608. Wind in the Willows, ca. 1930, iron, 6½", #12515, rarity 5*, $225.00.

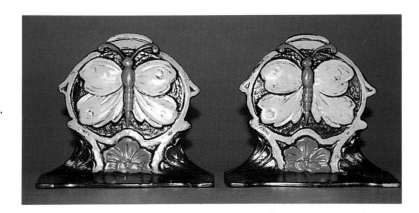

Plate 609. Butterfly, ca. 1925, iron, 5¼", rarity 4, $85.00.

Plate 610. Zinnias, ca. 1925, iron, 5¼", rarity 4, $60.00.

Plate 611. Bouquet, 1920, Ronson, gray metal, 6", LVA, 1920, rarity 5*, $125.00. (Ronson is one of the few makers to spend any time adding appeal to the bookrest aspect of bookends, as shown on this piece.)

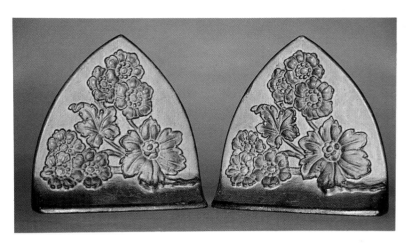

Plate 612. Flowers, 1922, Albany Foundry, iron, 9", rarity 5*, $150.00.

Plate 613. Floral Design, ca. 1925, brass, 6", rarity 3, $50.00.

Plate 614. Royal Fruit Bowl, ca. 1920, iron, 8½", rarity 5, $135.00.

Plate 615. Flower Basket, ca. 1925, Hubley, iron, 5¾", #8, rarity 4, $175.00. (Collection of Sue Benoliel)

Plate 616. Mixed Bouquet, ca. 1925, Albany Advertising Company, iron, 5¾", shopmark, rarity 5, $170.00. (Collection of Sue Benoliel)

Plate 617. Roses, ca. 1930, leather, approx. 5", rarity 4, $40.00.

Plate 618. Pine Needle, ca. 1914, Heintz Art Metal, bronze with silver overlay, shopmark, 5", rarity 5, $175.00 – 400.00. (Collection of David Surgan)

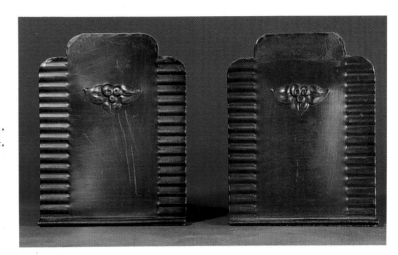

Plate 619. Tri-berry, ca. 1935, Craftsman, Inc., copper, 5", shopmark, #269, handmade, rarity 4, $50.00.

Plate 620. Bamboo, ca. 1914, Heintz Art Metal, bronze with silver overlay, shopmark, 5", rarity 5, $175.00 – 400.00. (Collection of David Surgan)

Plate 621. Pine Cone, ca. 1914, Heintz Art Metal, bronze with silver overlay, shopmark, 5", rarity 5, $175.00 – 400.00. (Collection of David Surgan)

Plate 622. Flowered Mantle, ca. 1914, Heintz Art Metal, bronze with silver overlay, shopmark, 5¼", rarity 5, $175.00 – 400.00. (Collection of David Surgan)

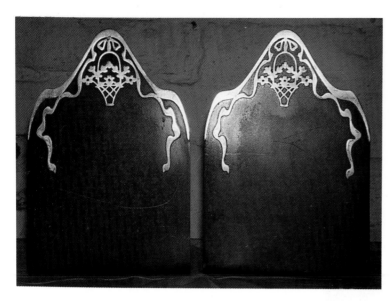

Plate 623. Basket of Flowers, ca. 1914, Heintz Art Metal, bronze with silver overlay, shopmark, 5¼", rarity 4, $175.00 – 400.00. (Collection of David Surgan)

Plate 624. Poppy, ca. 1915, Heintz Art Metal, bronze with silver overlay on expandable oak base, shopmark, 5", rarity 5, $175.00 – 400.00. (Collection of David Surgan)

Plate 625. Date Palm, ca. 1924, Heintz Art Metal Works, bronze (green patina) with silver overlay, shopmark, rarity 5, $175.00 – 425.00. (Collection of David Surgan)

Plate 626. Toadstool and Frog, ca. 1922, McClelland Barclay, gray metal, 4¼", rarity 5, $195.00. Other finishes seen include green/bronze.

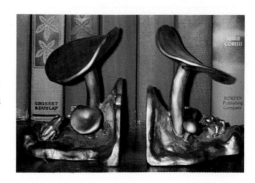

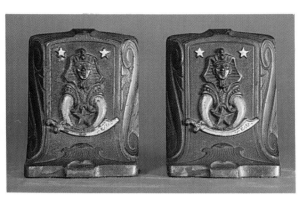

Plate 627. Shriners and Stars, ca. 1925, Judd, iron, 5¼", rarity 4, $110.00.

Plate 628. Shriner Fez, 1922, Ronson, gray metal, 3¼", LV Aronson 1922, rarity 3, $75.00. (Collection of Richard Weinstein)

Plate 629. Shriner Saber, ca. 1920, iron, 4¾", rarity 5, $85.00.

Plate 630. Brass Shriners, ca. 1935, Robins Co., brass, 5½", shopmark (Attleboro), rarity 5, $85.00.

Plate 632. Shriner Camel, ca. 1930, brass, 4½", rarity 5, $110.00. (Courtesy Kay Ross's White Elephant Antiques, Dallas)

Plate 631. Shriner Crescent, 1922, Ronson, gray metal, 3¼", LV Aronson 1922, rarity 4, $95.00. (Collection of Richard Weinstein)

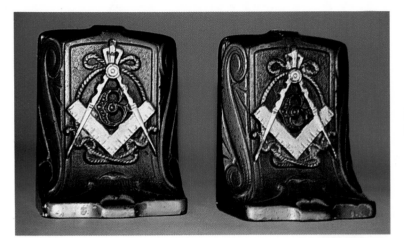

Plate 633. Masons, ca. 1920, Judd, iron, 5¼", rarity 5, $115.00.

Plate 634. Masonic Emblem, ca. 1928, Judd, iron, 5¼", rarity 4, $100.00.

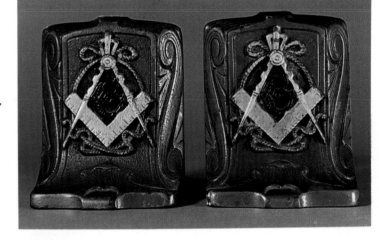

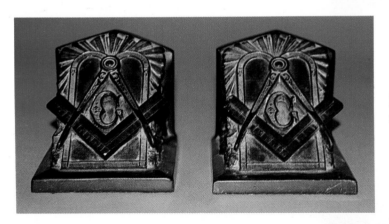

Plate 635. Masons (Ronson), 1922, Ronson, gray metal, 4¼", LV Aronson, 1922, rarity 5, $95.00.

Plate 636. Knights of Columbus, 1922, Ronson, gray metal, 3¼", LV Aronson 1922, rarity 3, $85.00.

Plate 637. Eastern Star, 1922, Ronson, gray metal, 4¼", LV Aronson, 1922, rarity 5, $125.00 (in black polychrome, rarity 4, $100.00).

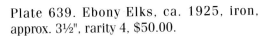

Plate 638. Moose Lodge, 1922, Ronson, gray metal, 4¼", LV Aronson, 1922, rarity 5, $125.00.

Plate 639. Ebony Elks, ca. 1925, iron, approx. 3½", rarity 4, $50.00.

Plate 640. BPOE Design, 1922, Ronson, gray metal, 3¼", LV Aronson 1922, rarity 3, $75.00.

Plate 641. Oddfellows, ca. 1935, Vergne Artware (West Coast Industries, Oakland, California), #119, bronze, 6¼", rarity 4, $125.00.

Plate 642. American Legion, ca. 1939, bronze, approx. 8", rarity 5, $115.00.

Plate 643. Syria Temple, ca. 1930, gray metal, approx. 5½", rarity 5, $75.00.

Plate 644. Scottish Rite, 1922, Ronson, gray metal, 3¼", LV Aronson, rarity 3, $85.00.

Plate 645. OAC, 1947, iron, approx. 5½", rarity 5, $75.00.

Plate 646. Elks, ca. 1920, Judd, iron, 5¼", rarity 5, $115.00.

Plate 647. Cherub and Butterfly, ca. 1924, Ronson, gray metal, company tag #7072, 6¼", rarity 4 (black), 5 (polychrome), $175.00 (black), $200.00 (polychrome).

Plate 648. Cherub, ca. 1925, Verona, iron, 8", shopmark, rarity 5, $210.00.

Plate 649. I'se Comin, ca. 1923, gray metal, 5¾", rarity 5*, $175.00.

Plate 650. Cherub Reading, ca. 1925, attr. Armor Bronze, bronze clad, approx. 6", sculptor signature S. Morani, rarity 5, $150.00.

Plate 651. Moon Rabbit, ca. 1935, brass, 5", rarity 5*, $110.00.

Plate 652. Camel Rack, ca. 1928, attr. Judd, brass, 5¼", rarity 4, $145.00.

Plate 653. Sleeping Fox, ca. 1930, gray metal, approx. 4", rarity 5, $125.00. (Courtesy Kay Ross's White Elephant Antiques, Dallas)

Plate 654. Thirsty Camel, ca. 1925, bronze clad, 6½" rarity 5, $125.00. (Courtesy Jay Mendlovitz)

Plate 655. Buffalo, 1923, Ronson, gray metal, 4¼", LV Aronson, 1923, rarity 5*, $225.00.

Plate 656. Arielle's Ark, 1996, Arielle Kuritzky, age 14, chalk, 5½", rarity 5*, priceless.

Plate 657. Buffalo Hunt, ca. 1930, bronze, approx. 5½", rarity 4, $150.00.

Plate 658. Alaskan Inhabitants, 1978, Washington Mint, Inc., marbelloid, 6½", rarity 3, $85.00.

Plate 659. Bear and Beehive, ca. 1940, pewter, 8", rarity 5, $100.00.

Plate 660. Looney Tunes, 1994, Disney, chalk, approx. 7", rarity 4, $85.00.

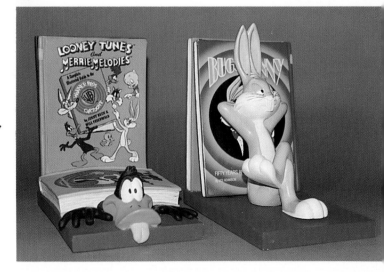

Lincoln Imp

The Lincoln Cathedral of Lincoln, England is one of the least known of the great European cathedrals, built mainly 1072 – 1280. At the peak of its development, it was literally taller than the Great Pyramids! Technically, a cathedral is a church that contains a bishop's seat, or cathedra. In April of 1185 the church was largely destroyed by an earthquake.

The imp of the Lincoln cathedral probably developed its notoriety because of its proximity to the St. Hugh's Head Shrine, directly above the shrine. Bishop Hugh was sainted in 1220, "as a result of presentation of miracles performed by him before, during, and after his death." A substantial number of pilgrimage patrons (the highest recorded number of persons visiting a pilgrimage site in England) came to the cathedral, and visited the shrine of St. Hugh. The legend of the Lincoln Imp, as provided from the Cathedral, goes as follows: "One day many years ago, the wind, being in a playful mood, brought two imps to see Lincoln. The first thing that attracted their attention on drawing near the City was its magnificent Minster. They were filled with awe and astonishment at so noble a building and it caused their hearts to sink within them for a time, but plucking up courage, they flew thither to more closely examine its wonderful carvings and mouldings. After flying around for some hours, one Imp found the South door open and, with great trepidation, impishly popped his head inside. Catching sight of the exquisite Angel Choir, he could not resist the temptation of a chat with the angels, so in he hopped, making straight for a pillar. He hopped still higher, but his curiosity cost him dear, for no sooner had he reached the top to rest, than he was, in a moment, turned to stone. The other Imp, tired of looking for his lost brother, alighted on the back of a witch. He was also immediately turned to stone. The wind still haunts the Minster Close, awaiting the return of the two imps."

More recently, in 1896 King Edward VII, then Prince of Wales, wore a gold imp scarf pin while riding his horse Persimmon to win the Derby, adding to the notoriety of the Lincoln figure.

Reference: "Lincoln Cathedral," English Life Publication, Inc., Derby, England.

Plate 661. Lincoln Imp, ca. 1926, bronze, 4¼", Lincoln Imp, 1255, rarity 5, $110.00.

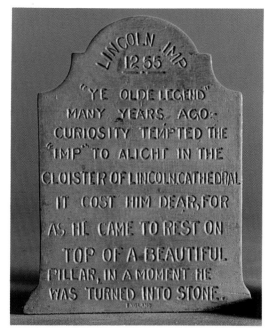

Plate 661A. Same as above, showing text inscription on reverse.

Plate 662. Ye Olde Inn, ca. 1940, Syroco Wood, company tag, 6¼", rarity 3, $45.00.

Plate 663. Shopmark of Syroco Wood (Syracuse Ornamental Corporation).

Plate 664. The Alamo, 1930, Alamo Iron Works Safety, iron, 4¼", Alamo Iron Works Safety, 4/1/30, rarity 5, $195.00. (Courtesy Jay Mendlovitz)

Plate 665. Forest Cabin, ca. 1922, Albany Foundry, iron, (hand painted, each may be slightly different), Albany, NY, rarity 3, $70.00.

Plate 666. Berkshire Symphonic Music Shed, ca. 1925, iron, 4½", Berkshire Symphonic Music Shed, rarity 5, $100.00

Plate 667. Church, ca. 1925, iron, 9", rarity 5, $75.00.

Plate 668. Christian Science Building, New York World's Fair, 1939, brass, 4¼", rarity 4, $95.00.

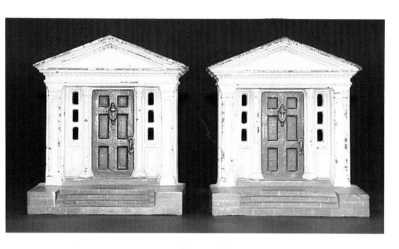

Plate 669. Door, ca. 1925, iron, 6", rarity 5 (polychrome), 4 (other finishes), $130.00 (polychrome), $100.00 (other finishes).

Plate 670. Stained Glass, ca. 1925, Bradley and Hubbard, iron with stained glass inside, 5½", shopmark (the outer plate must be removed to see the shopmark in the iron), rarity 5*, $225.00.

Plate 671. NCR Schoolhouse, showing reverse markings, 1931, brass, 4⅞", The NCR Schoolhouse, rarity 5*, $550.00.

Plate 672. Old Stagecoach, 1934 (pictured in Wallenstein & Meyer catalog, 1934), iron, 4", rarity 4, $95.00.

Plate 673. The Mill, ca. 1925, Verona, iron, 6¾", shopmark, rarity 4, $60.00.

Plate 674. Country Cottage, ca. 1924, Hubley, iron, 5½", rarity 3, $70.00.

Plate 675. Castle Lichtenstein, ca. 1925, Bradley and Hubbard, iron, 5", shopmark, rarity 5*, $150.00.

Plate 676. Church in Archway, ca. 1925, iron, approx. 5", rarity 4, $110.00.

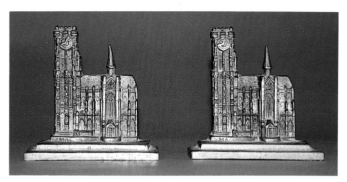

Plate 677. Church with Spire, ca. 1925, MTV, iron, 4¼", rarity 4, $50.00.

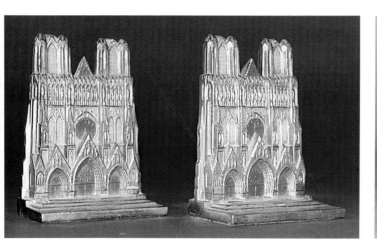

Plate 678. Cathedral, ca. 1927, Ronson, gray metal, 5½", company tag #11485, rarity 4, $115.00 (polychrome), $90.00 (other finishes).

Plate 679. The Front Door, ca. 1925, Bradley and Hubbard, iron, 5¾", rarity 4, $125.00. (Not pictured, gray and white finish, rarity 5, $175.00.)

Plate 680. Church Doors, ca. 1925, attr. Moffat, iron, 6", #9737, rarity 4, $175.00.

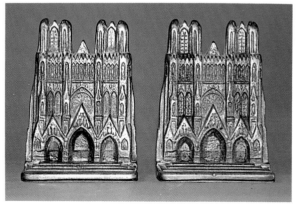

Plate 681. Bishop's Cathedral, ca. 1929, iron, 5½", rarity 3, $45.00.

Plate 682. Country Gate, ca. 1935, Bradley and Hubbard, 5", shopmark, iron, rarity 5, $125.00.

Plate 683. Shopmark (company tag), Bradley and Hubbard.

Plate 684. Oaken Door, ca. 1975, wood with metal ring, rarity 2, $15.00.

Plate 685. Baby Shoes, 1940, gray metal, 5½", Pat. 1940, rarity 4, $75.00.

Plate 686. Key, ca. 1935, brass, 8",
rarity 4, $75.00.

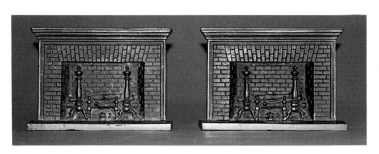

Plate 687. Fireplace, ca. 1925, Solid Bronze, iron, 4",
shopmark, rarity 4, $115.00.

Plate 688. Home's Hearth, ca. 1935, approx. 6",
bronze, rarity 5*, $300.00. (Courtesy John Asfor)

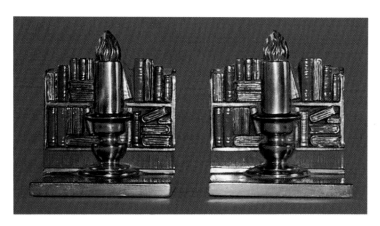

Plate 689. Volumes and Candlelight, ca. 1930, Ronson,
gray metal, 4¼", company tag #11484, rarity 4 (polychrome), 3 (other finishes), $90.00 (polychrome),
$65.00 (other finishes).

Plate 690. Hall's Bookcase, 1928, S.W. Hall, Bakelite, 5¾", design copyrighted Sept. 1928, Samuel W. Hall, rarity 5*, $350.00.

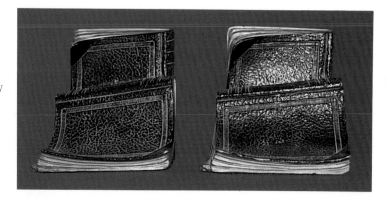

Plate 691. Limp-grained Leather, 1933, Ronson, gray metal, 4½", AMW 1933, rarity 3, $50.00.

Plate 692. Book, ca. 1930, Frankart, gray metal, 5½", shopmark, rarity 5*, $175.00. (These books are identical to those forming a pedestal for some Frankart deco girls; it is possible they have been altered, and the girls removed or damaged.)

Plate 693. Bacon and Johnson, ca. 1930, brass, 6½", rarity 4, $110.00.

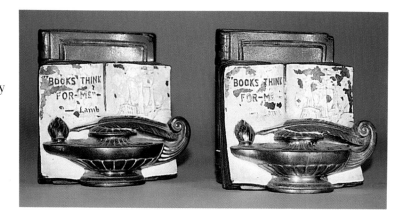

Plate 694. Lamp and Book, 1942, Ronson, gray metal, 5", LVA, 1942, rarity 4, $100.00.

Plate 695. Shakespeare Quote, ca. 1925, Bradley and Hubbard, iron, 6", shopmark, rarity 5, $150.00. (Collection of Sue Benoliel)

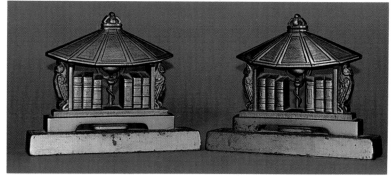

Plate 696. Lamp of Knowledge, ca. 1925, Judd, iron, 4¾", #9886, rarity 4, $100.00.

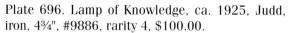

Plate 697. Ten Commandments, 1922, Ronson, gray metal, 3¾", LV Aronson, 1922, rarity 5*, $175.00.

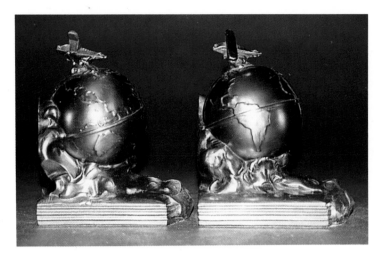

Plate 698. Around the World, ca. 1930, K&O, gray metal, 5¾", rarity 4, $100.00.

Plate 699. Icon, ca. 1930, iron, CHILE, 6", rarity 4, $75.00.

Plate 700. Tufts College, ca. 1970, iron, 6½", rarity 3, $60.00.

Plate 701. Cyclopedia of Medicine, ca. 1930, H.F. Grammes & Sons, Inc., brass, approx. 8", FA Davis, Co., rarity 5, $125.00.

Plate 702. Sajous' Cyclopedia, ca. 1925, iron, 6½",
rarity 5, $75.00.

Plate 703. Linden Hall, ca. 1960, gray metal,
approx. 3", rarity 5, $25.00.

Plate 704. Mayo Tunnel, ca. 1940, Mine
Equipment, Lancaster, Pennsylvania, iron, 5",
shopmark, rarity 5*, $75.00. (Collection of
Sue Benoliel)

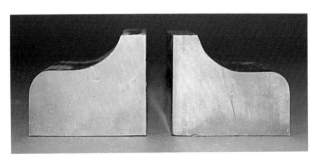

Plate 705. Cubic Symmetry, ca. 1935, bronze, 3",
rarity 5*, $110.00.

Plate 706. Truck, ca. 1925, iron, 5½", rarity 5, $195.00.

Plate 707. Covered Wagon, ca. 1926, W.H. Howell, iron, 4½", shopmark #14, rarity 4, $65.00.

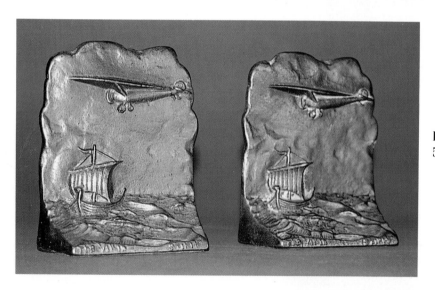

Plate 708. Viking Spirit, ca. 1928, iron, 5¼", rarity 5, $110.00.

Plate 709. Cogwheel, ca. 1965, brass, approx. 3½", rarity 5, $150.00.

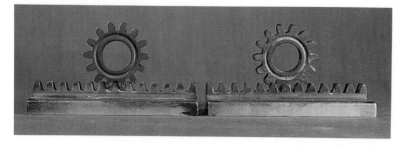

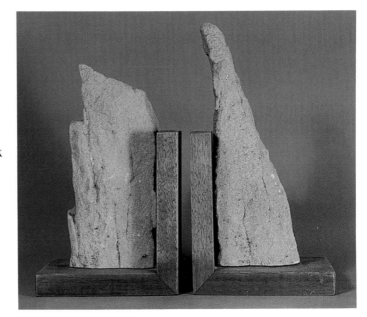

Plate 710. Zion Park, 1968, Zion Park Sandstone, rarity 3, $75.00.

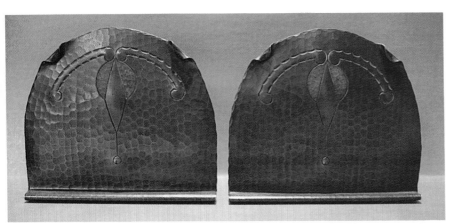

Plate 711. Hammered Arch Design, ca. 1914, Carl Soreson, copper, 5½", shopmark, rarity 4, $175.00. (Collection of Sue Benoliel)

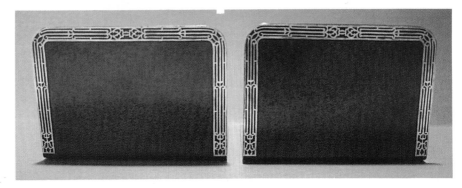

Plate 712. Heintz Geometric, ca. 1930, Heintz Art Metal, sterling silver on bronze, 4¼", rarity 5, $300.00. (Collection of Sue Benoliel)

Plate 713. Silvercrest Herald, ca. 1930, Silver Crest, silver on bronze, 4½", Silver Crest #8350, rarity 5, $125.00. (Collection of Sue Benoliel)

Plate 714. Signs of the Zodiac, ca. 1930, Tiffany, bronze, 5¼", shopmark, rarity 4, $400.00. (Collection of Sue Benoliel)

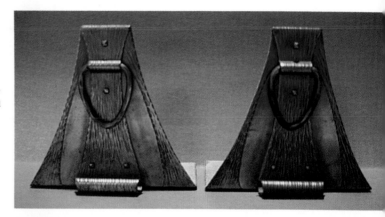

Plate 715. Triangle and Ring, ca. 1925, Roycroft, brass, 5", shopmark, rarity 4, $240.00. (Collection of Sue Benoliel)

Plate 716. Embossed Flower, ca. 1920, Roycroft, brass, 8½", shopmark, rarity 4, $350.00. One bookend is open on the end to allow viewing of the decorative cover of books of the time period. (Collection of Sue Benoliel)

Plate 717. Spiral, ca. 1920, Tiffany, bronze, approx. 6", shopmark, rarity 5, $500.00.

Plate 718. Cattail (left), ca. 1915, Heintz Art Metal, bronze with silver overlay, 5", shopmark, rarity 5, $175.00 – 400.00.* (Collection of David Surgan)
California Pepper (right), ca. 1915, Heintz Art Metal, bronze with silver overlay, 3", shopmark, rarity 5, $175.00 — 400.00.* (Collection of David Surgan)

Plate 719. Leaping Antelope, ca. 1915, Heintz Art Metal, bronze with silver overlay, 4¼", shopmark, rarity 5, $175.00 – 400.00.* (Collection of David Surgan)

Plate 720. Dogwood with Monogram (left), ca. 1914, Heintz Art Metal, bronze with silver overlay, 3", rarity 5, $175.00 – 400.00.* (Collection of David Surgan)
  Stylized Floral (right), ca. 1914, Heintz Art Metal, bronze, gold Doré patina, 3", rarity 5, $175.00 – 400.00.* (Collection of David Surgan)

Plate 721. Snake Charmer (left), ca. 1914, Heintz Art Metal, bronze and acid-etched silver, 3½", rarity 5, $175.00 – 400.00.* (Collection of David Surgan)
  Scrolled Wreath (center), ca. 1914, Heintz Art Metal, bronze with silver overlay, 3½", shopmark, rarity 5, $175.00 – 400.00.* (Collection of David Surgan)
  Butterfly Floral (right), ca. 1914, Heintz Art Metal, bronze with silver overlay, 3½", shopmark, rarity 5, $175.00 – 400.00.* (Collection of David Surgan)

*High degree of collectibility accounts for the wide price ranges of these Heintz Art Metal pieces. Collectors look especially at the nature and condition of pieces' patina.

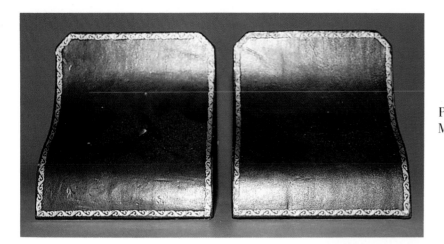

Plate 722. Leather Simplicity, ca. 1938, Pola Manufacturing Co., leather, 5", rarity 2, $35.00.

Plate 723. Florentine, ca. 1985, wood, 5¾", rarity 1, $15.00.

Plate 724. White Floral, ca. 1929, Harlich and Co., leather, Harlich & Co., Chicago, 5¾", rarity 4, $45.00.

Plate 725. Columns, 1922, Ronson, gray metal, 4½", LV Aronson, 1922, rarity 4, $50.00. (Collection of Richard Weinstein)

Plate 726. Ronson Conventional Scroll Design, ca. 1925, Ronson, gray metal, 4¼", company tag #10512, rarity 4, $75.00. (Collection of Richard Weinstein)

Plate 727. Pontiac, 1983, Bruce Fox, aluminum, company tag, New Albany, Indiana, rarity 5*, $50.00.

Plate 728. AYW, ca. 1920, iron, 5¾", rarity 5*, $110.00.

Plate 728A. Shopmark, Bruce Fox.

Plate 729. Child Reading, 1928, Frankart, gray metal, 6½", shopmark, rarity 5, $300.00.

Plate 730. Stars and Stripes, ca. 1935, brass, 4", rarity 5*, $110.00.

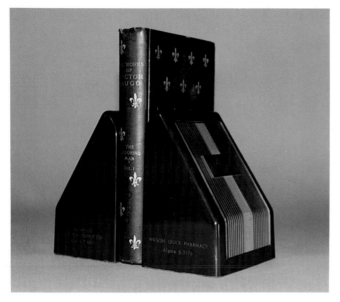

Plate 731. Nashville Surgical Supply Co., ca. 1930, B&B, Bakelite, 4¾", B&B Remembrance St. Paul Pat. #2284849, rarity 4, $50.00.

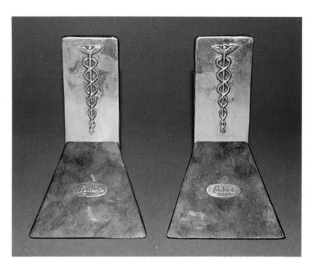

Plate 732. Lederle Caduceus, ca. 1995, Lederle, brass, 6", Lederle, rarity 4, $25.00.

Plate 733. 4-H, ca. 1930, brass, 5", rarity 5, $65.00.

Plate 734. Liberty Bell, ca. 1938, iron, approx 4½", rarity 2, $20.00.

Plate 735. Menorah, ca. 1935, iron, IOBB (attr. International Organization of B'nai Brith) 5", rarity 5, $75.00.

Plate 736. Dragon, 1949, Imperial Cathay Crystal, approx. 5", rarity 5, $400.00. (These are actually candle holders, a fact not immediately obvious; they have been mis-identified and used as bookends). (Collection of Michael Horseman)

Plate 737. Igloo, 1949, Glenmore Distilleries, aluminum, 5", shopmark (this item is registered as design patent #152,802, to Edgar Kelley, Jr., Kirkwood, Missouri, Feb. 22, 1949, assigned to Glenmore Distilleries Company, Louisville, Kentucky), rarity 5*, $295.00.

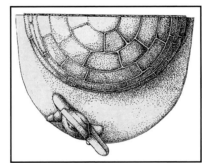

Design patent drawings for Igloo, Plate 737,

Plate 738. Decorative Scroll, ca. 1925, attr. Judd, iron, 5", rarity 5*, $200.00. (Courtesy Rhoda and Bernard Heyer, Let Bygones Be Antiques)

Plate 739. Iron Gate, ca. 1925, iron, approx. 5", rarity 5, $125.00. (Courtesy of Kay Ross's White Elephant Antiques, Dallas)

Plate 740. Seashell, ca. 1935, Revere, spring-coiled steel and resin composition, shopmark, rarity 3, $45.00.

Plate 741. Fencepost, ca. 1935, Revere, spring-coiled steel and resin composition, shopmark, rarity 3, $45.00.

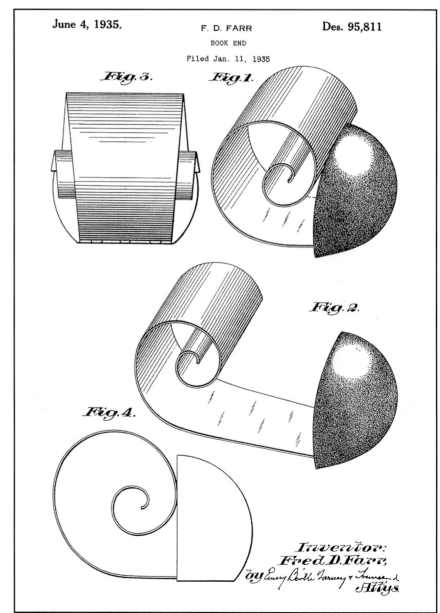

Design patent for the steel spring coil bookend design.

PATENTS

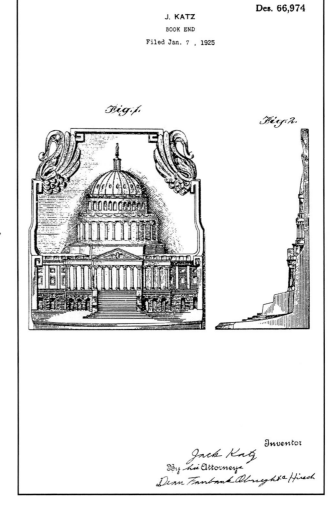

Capitol Building, ca. 1925, Jack Katz (patent registrant), rarity, patent only seen.

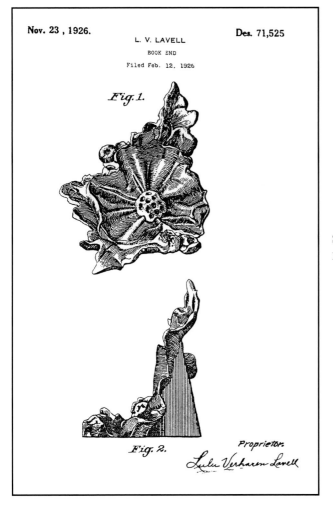

Single Blossom, ca. 1926, Lulu Lavell (patent registrant), gray metal, 5", rarity 4, $75.00.

March 15, 1927.

B. N. SKIFF

Des. 72,245

BOOK END OR SIMILAR ARTICLE

Filed Nov. 22. 1926

INVENTOR.
Bessie N. Skiff
BY
ATTORNEY.

Floral Motif, ca. 1927, B.N. Skiff (patent registrant), rarity, patent only seen.

Sept. 6, 1932.

C. A. HEDEGARD

Des. 87,718

BOOK END

Filed June 22, 1932

Fig.1

Fig.2

INVENTOR.
Clarence A. Hedegard

FRIENDS

Friends, ca. 1932, C.A. Hedegard (patent registrant), rarity, patent only seen.

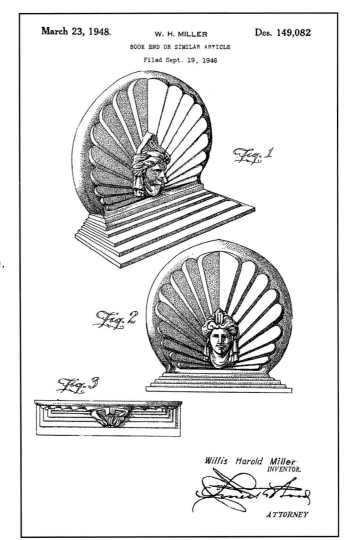

March 23, 1948. W. H. MILLER Des. 149,082

BOOK END OR SIMILAR ARTICLE

Filed Sept. 19, 1946

Fig. 1

Fig. 2

Fig. 3

Willis Harold Miller
INVENTOR.

ATTORNEY

Radiant Face, ca. 1948, W.H. Miller (patent registrant), rarity, patent only seen.

April 13, 1948. A. LEVA Des. 149,280

BOOK END

Filed Nov. 20, 1946

Fig. 1

Fig. 2

INVENTOR
ALEXANDER LEVA

BY

ATTORNEY

Two Kinds of Pups, ca. 1948, Alexander Leva (patent registrant), gray metal, 5", rarity 4, $110.00.

One Hand on the Wheel, ca. 1948, Alexander Leva (patent registrant), rarity, patent only seen.

Frog Fest, ca. 1951, L.T. Cardevaant (patent registrant), rarity, patent only seen.

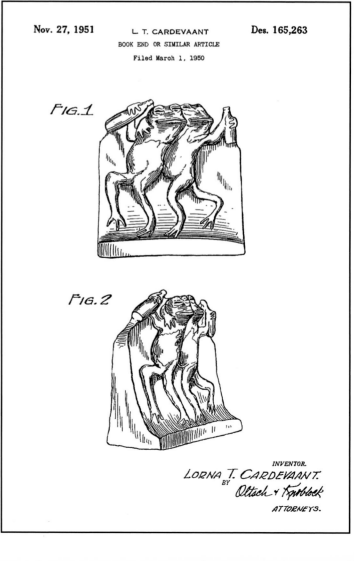

Reader of the Scroll, ca. 1920, Gorham, bronze, 8½",
Sculptor: N.J. Murphy.

Kneeling Men, ca. 1920, Gorham, bronze, 6½", Sculptor:
Isidore Konti.

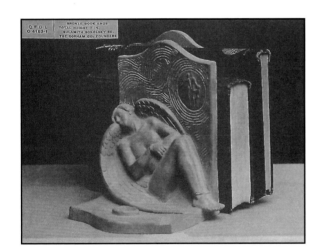

Angel in Repose, ca. 1920, Gorham, bronze, 7",
Sculptor: Sulamith Sokolsky.

Male Nude, ca. 1920, Gorham, bronze, 13½", Sculptor:
Edna I. Spencer.

Items in this section have only been seen in archival
photographs if rarity and value are not included in description.

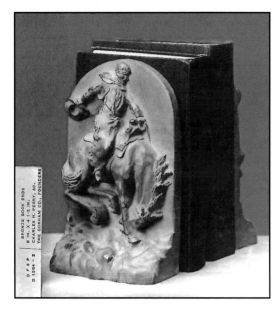

Bronco Buster, ca. 1920, Gorham, bronze, 8",
Sculptor: Charles M. Perry.

Golf Player, ca. 1920, Gorham, bronze, 6", Sculptor: T.B. Starr.

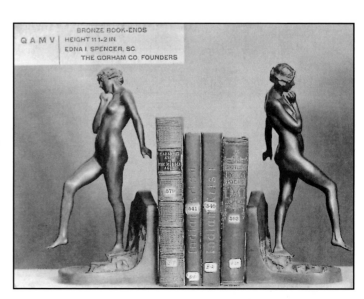

Workmen, ca. 1920, Gorham, bronze, 13",
Sculptor: E.E. Codman.

Stepping Lightly, ca. 1920, Gorham, bronze,
11½", Sculptor: Edna I. Spencer.

Thought and Progress, ca. 1920, Gorham, bronze, 10", Sculptor: Isidore Konti.

Thought Provoking, ca. 1920, Gorham, bronze, 6½", Sculptor: L. H. Treadway.

Reclining Lady, ca. 1920, Gorham, bronze, 9½", Sculptor: H. K. Bush-Brown.

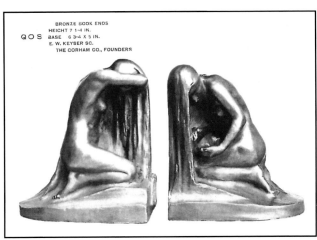

Long-haired Maiden, ca. 1920, Gorham, bronze, 7¼", Sculptor: E. W. Keyser.

Knowledge (Gorham), ca. 1920, Gorham, bronze, 6⅝", Sculptor: F. Ziegler.

Science and Knowledge, ca. 1920, Gorham, bronze, 6⅝", Sculptor: F. F. Ziegler.

Dancing Girl (Gorham), ca. 1920, Gorham, bronze, 6¾",
Sculptor: F. Ziegler, rarity 5, $450.00.

Meditation (Gorham), ca. 1920, Gorham,
bronze, Sculptor: E.E. Codman, 7".

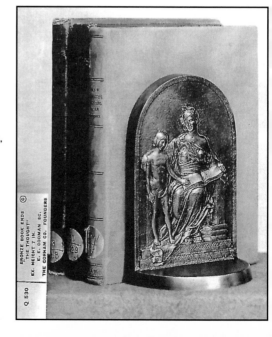

Learning, ca. 1920, Gorham, bronze, Sculptor: E.E.
Codman.

The Thought, ca. 1920, Gorham, bronze,
Sculptor: E.E. Codman, 7".

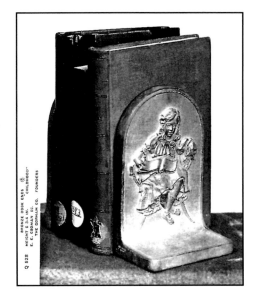

Childhood, ca. 1920, Gorham, bronze, 6¾", Sculptor, E.E. Codman.

Girl with Basket, ca. 1920, Gorham, bronze, 5¼", Sculptor: Margaret T. Meyers.

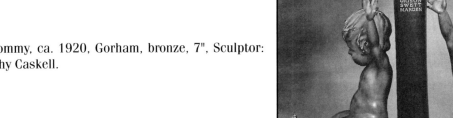

Up Mommy, ca. 1920, Gorham, bronze, 7", Sculptor: Dorothy Caskell.

Baby Asleep Under Tree, ca. 1920, Gorham, bronze, 5½", Sculptor: Dorothy Rich.

Growing Into My Hat, ca. 1920, Gorham, bronze, 7⅔", Sculptor: M.T. Bradley, artist signed.

Girl and Baby Doll, ca. 1920, Gorham, bronze, Sculptor: Burke.

Peek-a-boo, ca. 1920, Gorham, bronze, 5¾", Sculptor: E. B. Parsons.

Exploring Baby, ca. 1920, Gorham, bronze, 7", Sculptor: B. Putnam.

Faun and Mermaid, ca. 1920, Gorham, bronze, 5½", Sculptor: Louis Mayer.

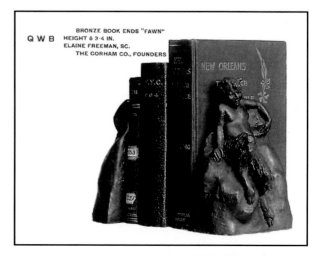

Fawn, ca. 1920, Gorham, bronze, 6¾", Sculptor: Elaine Freeman.

Colonial House, ca. 1920, Gorham, bronze, 7", FFZ, Sculptor, F. F. Zeigler.

Ears Up and Down, ca. 1920, Gorham, bronze, 8½", Sculptor: F. B. Cowdin.

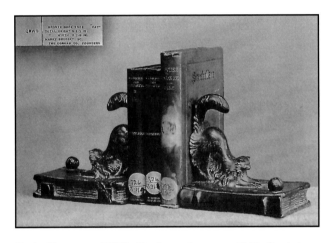

Cat's Play, ca. 1920, Gorham, bronze, 5½", Sculptor: Harry B. Rodsky.

Bull Terrier, ca. 1920, Gorham, bronze, 7¼", Sculptor: Edith Parsons.

Airedale (Parsons), ca. 1920, Gorham, bronze, 5½", Sculptor: Edith B. Parsons, rarity 5, $1,200.00.

Friskies, ca. 1920, Gorham, bronze, 5⅞", Sculptor: Ethel Ehrmann.

Just One More Cookie, Please, ca. 1920, Gorham, bronze, 7¼", Sculptor: E. Knauth.

Bull and Bear, ca. 1920, Gorham, bronze, 5¼".

Buffalo Skull, 1915, Gorham, bronze, 6¾" Sculptor: Henry N. Moeller.

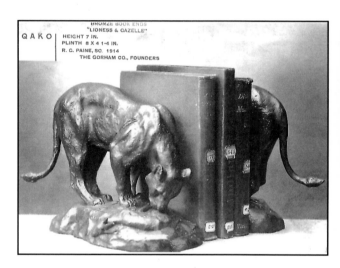

Lioness and Gazelle, 1914, Gorham, bronze, 8", Sculptor: R.C. Paine.

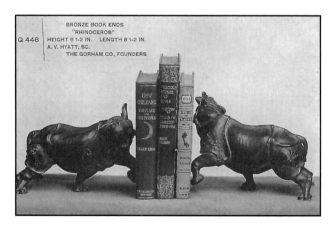

Rhinoceros, ca. 1920, Gorham, bronze, Sculptor: A.V. Hyatt.

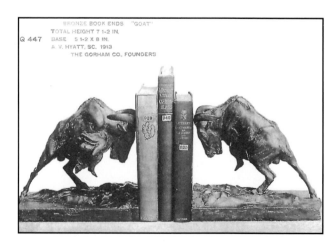

Goat, ca. 1913, Gorham, bronze, 7½", Sculptor: A.V. Hyatt.

THE COMPANIES
ARMOR BRONZE COMPANY

The Armor Bronze Company produced some pieces in their New York City location probably as early as 1919. From 1934 – 1964 the company operated in Taunton, Massachusetts, beginning with just four employees and its organizer George B. Collis. The company's official title in Taunton was Armor Bronze & Silver Company, though all the bookends seen to date have only been marked "Armor Bronze." From 1934 – 1958 the office was located on Spring Lane in Taunton; from 1952 – 1956 the factory was located at the corner of West Water Street and 4th Street. By 1964, the company had several hundred employees, and occupied 200,000 square feet of floor space in Taunton, but is last recorded doing business in 1969.

During World War II, the services of the company were directed to produce aircraft parts for Pratt-Whitney, but postwar production of silver hollow ware, copper, and brass gift items precipitated a separate division known as Coppercraft Guild in 1949. At this point, the company was the largest manufacturer of copper giftware in the world.

Armor Bronze is the most frequently seen manufacturer of bronze clad pieces. The company often chose well-known works of art and famous sculptures as material for their bookends. Only one piece has been seen in any other format than bronze clad: a cast gray metal Dante and Beatrice (Plate 235). Many pieces are artist-signed, and the colorful polychrome pieces they produced are some of the most artistically interesting products on the market.

Armor Bronze pieces have not been seen in solid bronze, and are often mistakenly thought to be "bronzes," but this term is usually reserved for works of solid bronze, or cast bronze pieces of sufficient metal thickness not to require supporting materials for structure. In most circumstances, the supporting plaster material with a central wick is clearly visible on the underside of the bookend; when the bottom is felt-covered, tapping against the side of the bookend reveals the separation between the outer layer of bronze and the underlying plaster.

BRADLEY AND HUBBARD MANUFACTURING COMPANY

The Bradley and Hubbard Manufacturing Company of Meriden, Connecticut, began as a partnership of Nathaniel L. Bradley and Walter Hubbard in 1854. Initially, they produced clocks, vases, mirror frames, tables, and other decorative metal articles. Later, oil lamps, and eventually, gas and electric light fixtures were manufactured by the company. Apparently well-known at the time, the Rayo Lamp was made for the Standard Oil Company by B & H. Elaborate chandeliers, candelabras, clocks, andirons, and even decorative clamp-on pincushions to be attached to a table-edge are depicted in their products produced in the 1854 – 1890 period. In 1940 B & H joined forces with the Charles Parker Company in Meriden, Connecticut. Parker had been developed in 1832, and was noted for lighting fixtures and architectural bronze and iron; what began as a popular market in Central and South America for its coffee mills spread later to the United States as it became fashionable to make freshly ground coffee in the home.

Nathaniel Bradley was born in Cheshire, Connecticut, Dec. 27, 1829, the youngest son of Levi and Abigail Ann (Atwater) Bradley, and was educated at an academy in Meriden. His first position was as a clerk with EBM Hughes, a hardware merchant in New Haven, Connecticut.

After one year at that position, Nathaniel was called home to assist on his parents' farm. Shortly after his return, a small lock factory in nearby Southington employed Nathaniel and his good work eventually elevated him to director and primary salesman for the company.

In 1852 a joint stock company was formed, Bradley, Hatch & Co., with $5,000 capital, and his brother Walter was a member of the firm. The first factory was a small wooden building without power, employing six persons. In January, 1875, the company became Bradley and Hubbard, Incorporated, with 150 employees (which expanded ultimately to employ 1,100), located at the corner of Hanover and Butler streets in Meriden. By 1892 offices and salesrooms were established in New York, Boston, Chicago, and Philadelphia.

Bradley was a very civic-minded individual. He was trustee of the Connecticut School for Boys for 14 years, after which he became president. Donation of a complete set of brass musical instruments made the dream of a school band a reality for the school. He contributed building funds for and was president of the Meriden Hospital. He was a member of the Connecticut Society of the Sons of the American Revolution. His philanthropy was noteworthy to the local YMCA, and to the Curtis Memorial Public Library of Meriden, which houses a bronze plaque of acknowledgment.

Walter Hubbard, born Sept. 23, 1828 in Middletown, Connecticut, was the other principal of B & H. His father was one of the original settlers of Middletown in 1650 from England, and like Nathaniel Bradley, Walter was raised on a farm. Hubbard opened a dry goods and clothing store in Meriden in 1851. In 1852 he married Abby Ann Bradley, sister of Nathaniel Bradley. Several months after their marriage, Abby died, and Hubbard never remarried. Hubbard served as president of Bradley and Hubbard from its time of incorporation for more than 30 years. Hubbard's philanthropy resulted in the building of New England's Winthrop Hotel. His community involvement included being a member of the Union League Club of New York, The New England Society of New York, and the American Geographical Society. He was fondly memorialized by the Hubbard and Meriden Park, in Meriden, Connecticut.

The works of Bradley and Hubbard are consistently excellent, and command consistently higher prices than comparable pieces. The vast majority of bookends are iron, though a few examples of bronze have been seen, and it is reported that some pieces were manufactured of cast gray metal. In contrast to many pieces which were apparently destined for more decor tive than functional careers, the majority of B&H bookends are of substantial weight and solidarity. The castings are often much greater detail than is seen from other manufacturers, and the polychrome paints are more colorful and enduring tha any other iron manufacturers. It is not at all uncommon to find B&H bookends with multicolored paint and shadings ful intact, even though they were produced in the 1920s. This is in stark contrast to many other iron pieces whose paint chi and corrodes much more readily. B&H pieces are sometimes marked with beige descriptive tags, on the underside, wi titles or brief descriptors of the subject matter, and are clearly marked with the B&H logo, as well as (rarely) the B&H co pany tag, a triangular identifying marker which also locates them in Meriden.

REFERENCE: 150 Years of Meriden: Published in Connection with the Observance of the City's Sesquicentennial June 17 – 2 1956.

A Century of Meriden "The Silver City", C. Bancroft Gillespie, Journal Publishing Co., Meriden, CT, 1906.

A History of New Haven County, J.H. Ronboy, Vol. 1, Chapter XI, "Meriden-Biographical Sketches," 1892.

ART & CRAFTS

The Arts and Crafts movement had its origins in Victorian England when John Ruskin, writer, art critic, and socia reformer, shared his ideas with people like his student William Morris. Morris's furnishing firm (Morris, Marshall, Faulkne & Co.) was established in 1861 and sold furniture, wallpaper, glassware, pottery, and other goods with an emphasis o quality of handcrafting.

In America in 1879, Associated Artists, founded by individuals like Louis Tiffany and Candace Wheeler, was formed, mod eled after the Morris company. At the same time, art potteries like Rookwood (1880, Cincinnati, Ohio) and others develope art pottery lines. In 1888 in England the Arts and Crafts Exhibition Society proposed the display of handcrafted goods.

Gustav Stickley in 1899 began United Crafts, which became Craftsmen Workshops in 1904, near Syracuse, New York His factory produced what is known as Mission style furniture.

Elbert Hubbard established Roycroft Shops in East Aurora, New York, in 1894, reportedly emulating William Morris's Kelmscott Press. Although initially directed to bookbinding and paper manufacture, the company expanded into meta work, lighting fixtures, and furniture.

CHASE
(CHASE MANUFACTURING COMPANY, CHASE COMPANIES, CHASE BRASS & COPPER COMPANY

Augustus Sabin Chase, founder of the Waterbury Manufacturing Company, was born Aug. 15, 1928, to farming parent Captain Seth and Eliza Hempstead Dodge Chase. In 1850, Chase moved to Waterbury to take a job with the only bank in tow by 1864 he was president of that bank.

In 1876 Chase and co-investors began the Waterbury Manufacturing Company with a group investment of $25,000. Initi products included buttons, pins, umbrella furniture, and a variety of brass castings. Employees worked 6 days a week, hours a day, earning from $1.00 – $3.00 daily.

At his death in 1896, A.S. Chase was succeeded as president by his son, Henry Sabin Chase. As a result of significan expanded brass business, in 1900 the company established its own brass mill, Chase Rolling Mill. During the early years the company, a great deal of notoriety was attributed to the company's use of Percheron horse teams for movement of hea equipment; the company at one time owned as many as 350 of these animals. In 1910, construction of Chase Metal Work began, which made significant contributions to the war effort in World War I. During the War, the U.S. government was th primary customer of Chase Metal Works, which required a major post-war redirection to commercial customers. Frederick Chase, successor as president to his brother, developed warehouses on both coasts, and in 1929 built an additional mill Cleveland, Ohio. Subsequently the company became a subsidiary of Kennecott Copper Corporation, at the time the worl largest producer of copper.

The company was initially known as Waterbury Manufacturing Company (1876), then as Chase Companies (until 1918 and finally in 1936, was incorporated as Chase Brass & Copper. Although there are no direct details available about even leading to the eventual demise, in the 1970s the local Waterbury paper commented on strikers at the local plant, and th imminent company liquidation.

The initial trademark of Chase was a diamond with the word "Chase" in the center. On Oct. 2, 1928, the company intr duced what came to be the trademark with which collectors generally identify Chase pieces: the half-man, half-horse arch (Chase centaur). In designing the piece, the body of the Percheron was chosen as the prototype.

In the prime of its success, Chase had offices and shops around the country. In their 1941 catalog, their office on th 46th floor of the Chase Tower at 10 E. 40th Street, New York City, is depicted, as well as a typical Chase shop: a display se tion containing a variety of Chase products, such as lamps, kitchen utensils, bookends, and the like. At the time, Cha shops were found both in small stores and large department stores such as May Company and Marshall Field's.

REFERENCE: *Art Deco Chrome, The Chase Era*, Richard Kilbride Jo-D Books, Stamford, CT, 1988.
Art Deco Chrome Book 2, Richard Kilbride, Jo-D Books, Stamford, CT, 1992.

THE CONNECTICUT FOUNDRY

The Connecticut Foundry, of Rocky Hill, Connecticut, was one of the most prolific bookend producers, and anyone with even passing interest in bookends will have encountered many of their pieces. Fortunately, almost all CF pieces are marked and dated, but usually with the company logo (a "C" inside a triangle, inside a circle, sometimes mistaken for a copyright symbol), rather than the name of the company. Occasionally, the pieces will be marked differently on each piece of the bookend pair, for instance, one will be imprinted "The Connecticut Foundry," and its partner will be marked with the company logo. Other variations exist. With one exception, The Aviator (Plate 106), all pieces have been identified produced in cast iron only, with no added paint. The Aviator has been seen as a single example in bronze. At least a few of the pieces were produced using the sand casting method, which results in pieces with some irregularities on the surface, and relative lack of detail, compared to other methods.

The earliest bookend copyright recorded for CF is May 4, 1928, and the last is March 11, 1929. During this period, 29 different pieces were copyrighted, all but a few of which have been seen and confirmed. It is unknown what other metal art works were produced by CF.

CRESCENT METAL WORKS

Crescent produced bookends of cast gray metal. The company incorporated in Newark, New Jersey Nov. 19, 1924, and voided their corporate status Jan. 13, 1937. Several of their pieces are especially elegant, and their female deco figures are characterized by lithe gracefulness. The registered agent of the company was Samuel S. Ferster, and the company was originally located at 800 Broad Street, Newark, but at least in 1929, John Skiba obtained a copyright while the business was located at 313 Chestnut Street, Newark.

DODGE, INC.

Company tags identify Dodge offices existing in Newark, Los Angeles, and Miami. The U.S. Patent Office possesses a copy of the company brochure received Aug. 10, 1948, which depicts what the company calls "the master line of gifts....designed for the discriminating buyer." In 1948, one office was located at 126 South Street, Newark. Five primary finishes were used for their cast gray metal pieces: SunRay (gold colored), Silver Plate (silver, with an intended oxidized look), Diamond Black (ebony), Antique Bronze (traditional high gloss bronze finish with two-tone highlights), and Combination (muted bronze in combination with SunRay).

In addition to bookends, Dodge made pipe rests, holders for book matches, ashtrays, figurines, lamps, desk novelties, and other pieces. The 1948 catalog lists more than 20 different pairs of bookends, including numerous pieces by the designer McClelland Barclay. To date, all pieces identified as Dodge are made of cast gray metal. Pieces on onyx bases are distinctly less common. In the 1940s, bookends sold for $10 – 40 per pair.

FLEURON, INC.

Fleuron, Inc. was established in the 1920s in North Tonawanda, New York, housed at 73-79 Robinson Street. The earliest business listing for Fleuron Corporation in 1928 showed A. L. Hyde as president and Frank L. Moore as vice president. The company probably ceased business in 1933, since in 1934 a new company called Kobbe Pottery, named after its originator Alexander Kobos, took up residence at that address. Additionally, none of the principals whose names had been previously attached to Fleuron were listed in association with Kobbe. By 1935 both Fleuron and its successor Kobbe are absent from the business community. Fleuron is registered as a producer of synthetic marble and pottery. In 1995, former employees of the Fleuron Company conveyed that the product itself was made from sulfur and a special type of sand. The sulfur was heated to a liquid stage and then sand was added. If color was desired, dye was mixed in. Once cooled, the mixture hardened rapidly to a marble-like substance.

The full spectrum of products produced by Fleuron is unknown, but several sets of bookends have been seen, and a flower pot and saucer made of Fleuron are part of the Historical Society of the Tonawandas collection. The bookends have a flat patina, a smooth-finished surface not unlike marble but much warmer, and have been seen in pale green (three examples) and beige (one example). The example shown here, Plate 301, is obviously taken from the same mold as Plate 302. The other examples have been busts of females. The material is of substantial weight, but chips easily like pottery, so pieces in good condition are difficult to find.

FRANKART

Arthur von Frankenberg, president and art director of Frankart, Inc., prolifically produced a diversity of metal crafted deco styled pieces. Although not known for detail, the lines and styling typify the Art Deco mode. In 1921 Frankart produced the first made as a candle holder, more Art Nouveau than Art Deco. Through the Depression, Frankart produced a wide variety of pieces, including candle holders, ashtrays, bookends, card holders, fishbowl stands, fruit bowls, candy dishes, and vase holders. Even chromium deco wall plaques were produced by Frankart. Von Frankbenburg himself was the sculptor of many of the pieces.

Almost all Frankart pieces are imprinted "Frankart, Pat. appld. for," yet only a few patents exist in the U.S. patent library record ed to Frankart. The earliest copyright recorded to Frankart is in 1925, for "Joy of Life" bookends, and copyrights continue to b recorded as late as 1928.

THE GIFT HOUSE

Little is known about the origins or final disposition of The Gift House, Inc. (New York 9/29/21 – 4/17/34) At one tim there was an apparent liaison between them and Nuart of New York (see section on Nuart). Pieces have thus far been see produced only in iron, and copyright records indicate product development as early as 1924, but the company's last copy right is recorded in 1926. Gift House bookends seen to date have the company name and date imprinted on the piece. Office were located at 10 East 15th Street, New York, in 1924, but moved to 14 West 23rd Street in 1926. Most of the company copyrights are issued to Salvatore Reina.

THE GORHAM COMPANY

The Gorham Company was founded by Jabez Gorham in 1831 in Providence, Rhode Island. Initially, the company pro duced small silver items, especially teaspoons. Small bronzes were made about 1860, but it was not until 1885 that the firs large nonecclesiastical bronze sculpture was produced ("The Skirmisher," a Civil War monument by Frederick Kohlhagen). separate bronze division was started about 1890.

HEINTZ ART METAL

The Heintz Art Metal shop was established by Otto L. Heintz in Buffalo, New York. He was the son of Louis Heintz, half of th old Buffalo manufacturing jewelry firm of Heintz Brothers. By 1903, Otto had purchased and was proprietor of Art Crafts Shop and had received the first of his patents. This was for enameled jewelry, utilizing silver webs to create the cavities to hold the di ferent colored enamel powders. By 1906, he had changed the company name to the Heintz Art Metal Shop, and shifted his focu from enamels toward sterling silver as ornamentation, and from copper to bronze as the base material.

By June 1911, Otto had perfected and applied for a patent covering his invention of a means of applying the silver withou solder to the base metal, and on August 27, 1912, U.S. Patent #1,037,143 for a "method of producing metallic articles" wa awarded to him. Items thus produced — vases, bowls, smoker's and desk sets, candlesticks, lamps, trophy cups and bookend were from that date forward marked with the conjoined letters HAMS enclosed in a diamond, below which the words "STERLIN ON BRONZE, PAT. AUG. 27.12" appeared. Bookends usually had a four-digit number, 71xx to 72xx, denoting shape, size, an style. Often a letter suffix denoted which silver overlay was used. Different hot chemical patinas, most notably mottled brown variegated green, or "Royal" (iridescent red) were utilized as well as plated finishes such as acid-etched silver, gold doré, an hand-stippled "French Grey."

A pair of bookends, circa 1914, was priced from $3.70 and was marketed through better art and giftware stores and large depar ment stores. Heintz ware made popular wedding gifts. A showroom was maintained at 6 West 40th Street in New York City, and R.I Macy was its largest retail outlet.

Much Heintz ware today has been severely compromised by ill-advised cleaning or attempts to polish the originally lacquere silver overlays, thus destroying the patinas. Consult an expert on Heintz ware before attempting any cleaning or polishing.

Heintz Art Metal Shop suffered a severe one-two punch with the death of 41-year-old Otto on January 10, 1918, and th defection of sales manager Fred Smith and some major craftsmen to their newly formed Smith Metal Arts Company, incorporate April 24, 1919. Heintz continued for another 10 years, steadily losing money, until the end came February 11, 1930, in the mids of the Great Depression. Today, the silver-on-patinated-bronze look is unique, unmistakably Heintz's, and avidly collected.

Contributed by David Surgan

J.B. HIRSCH FOUNDRY

J.B. Hirsch Foundry history begins with Joseph B. Hirsch's work with lead and tin in his homeland, Romania. In the ear 1900s, Hirsch immigrated to the US, and after brief employment with Con-Edison as a tinsmith, began his own company, orig nally called The New York Art Bronze Works which soon became one of the country's largest manufacturers of bookends. Th company was originally located on East 17th Street, in Manhattan. At the time, it was not uncommon for distributors and gi jobbers to import French statuary used as newel post lamps at the bottom of banisters. Often, these pieces arrived in need c repair, which was also a part of Hirsch's metalsmithing ability. Soon after this business demonstrated its potential for suc cess, he began to import his own pieces directly from French foundries, and after World War I when French occupation close one of his primary suppliers, he went to Paris and purchased that company's molds to begin his own casting foundry.

Subsequent acquisition of French, German, and Italian bronze molds resulted in what has been regarded as the larges finest and rarest collection of these items in the world, reported valued at over two million dollars.

World War II produced some surprising changes for the foundry, as French foundries hid their Beaux Arts molds in ce lars to avoid plunder from invading armies, and subsequent utilization of the metals for conversion into war materials. Part c the evasion process included breaking the molds into many small fragments, scrambling them, and hiding them underground.

It was not until 1948 that Abe Hirsch, son of Joseph, who by that time was managing the family business, went to Paris t y to resurrect these works of art. Abe personally spent days digging, pulling up floorboards, or moving heavy bins, searching r hidden caches of old bronze works. Abe's son Stanley, a recent college graduate, was placed in charge of re-assembling humed molds that arrived in various pieces. Over the next 15 years, multiple trips abroad resulted in the acquisition of comete molds of over 100 subjects, as well as numerous unidentified pieces, or incomplete molds.

Serendipity propelled the next step of company development. Stanley Hirsch attended a symposium on the Beaux Arts esented at the New York Metropolitan Museum of Art. Stanley was surprised to note that he had in his possession the origal molds from which the pieces on display were cast! When Hirsch consulted the curator of the Western European section the museum, he was linked up with Harold Berman, author.

Berman was so impressed with the Hirsch pieces, he obtained permission from the company to include 40 examples of eir pieces in his next volume of the bronze encyclopedia, and planted the suggestion that in addition to their focus on mps, they might consider producing limited editions of their remarkable French pieces, which has subsequently been a ajor interest of the company, and continues today.

Many Hirsch pieces are marked with their logo, and some are dated, but oftentimes the only clue to the maker is the tyle of the piece. As you will note from the photographs, Hirsch pieces are often romantic, elaborate, and elegantly esigned. To date, only figural pieces have been seen. Most of the pieces are cast in pure spelter, and often they reflect the hryselephantine movement, displaying ivorine (celluloid) faces, hands or other parts. Sometimes the figures are entirely etal (spelter) with parts painted to resemble ivorine.

Beethoven (Plate 596) and the Cellists (Plate 597) are two of the most popular Hirsch pieces. Some of their figural ieces are also seen in plaster; these pieces were made from the same molds as the original metal pieces, but when metal hortages and wartime demand diverted metals to other uses, plaster was substituted.

HUBLEY

The Hubley Manufacturing Company began in Lancaster, Pennsylvania, in 1894, and is most well known for its production f iron toys. In 1965 the company became part of Gabriel Industries, which continued to use the Hubley name until 1978. In ddition to numerous interesting bookends, Hubley produced ashtrays, banks, clocks, cage hooks, curtain hold-backs, button lates, door knockers, doorstops, place card holders, pet feeding dishes, desk novelties, and art novelties. Many of their booknds reflected popular artwork or sculpture ("Washington at Valley Forge", "End of the Trail", "Angelus Call to Prayer", "St. eorge and the Dragon"). Representative artists or sculptors associated with their pieces include G.G. Drayton (twin cat oorstop, puppy bank), and Fred Everett (doorstops depicting fowl). Flowers were the single subject portrayed with the greatst frequency in doorsteps. When considering bookends, dogs were their most widely utilized subject matter. Many pieces ame in more than one finish, but unfortunately, many of the pieces suffer great loss of painted finish over time. One of the ost colorful is "Serenade Tonight," (Plate 595) which comes in a delightful polychrome, or a very attractive bronze finish. Most ieces were completed in iron, but some in bronze also. Hubley bookends are generally imprinted with a two or three digit numer on the back, but no specific company logo. A single example of a Hubley company tag, a one centimeter diameter circular reen paper tag with the company name, has been found on their wirehaired terrier bookends.

JENNINGS BROTHERS

Jennings Brothers, usually known as "JB" among bookend enthusiasts, was begun about 1891 in Bridgeport, Conn., by dward Austin Jennings. The Jennings Brothers Manufacturing Company evolved into a multigeneration business which proided some of the most finely crafted art metal pieces existing today. Their typical methods of production required meticuous techniques which did not lend themselves well to machine-directed mass production, but rather depended upon the irect handiwork of expert artists, sculptors, and metal craftsmen. By the late 1940s, procuring such artists and utilizing heir techniques were of such economic burden to art metal crafters that monetary survival became a precarious situation.

E.A. Jennings (Jan. 8, 1963 – Sept. 13, 1952) was born in Greens Farms, Conn. He was educated at Greens Farms cademy and Park Avenue Institute. His first employment was with G.W. Barker (Bridgeport), followed by 10 years employent with the National Bank of Bridgeport and the Consolidated Rolling Stock Company. In 1888 the American Jewelry Comany was founded by Edward and his brother Erwin, which was re-organized and renamed Jennings Brothers Manufacturing ompany several years later. The first formal listing of JB as a business appears in the 1892 Bridgeport City Directory, and he last listing was in the 1953 directory. The Bridgeport Directory of 1929 states that the company was incorporated in 896 with a capital of $400,000; according to one grandson, this sum was put up by Edward's first wife and the wife of enry Jennings, one of Edward's brothers. The business was located at 219 Elm Street from 1905 when the Bridgeport Gun mplement Company building was purchased. At that time the company was known also as a major silver manufacturer. In 953 the site was purchased by James J. Sullivan, with the intention of razing the edifice to provide a parking lot, which was ubsequently accomplished in 1954.

The company prospered under the leadership of successive family members, including E.A. Jennings's son, Henry Ashton ennings. When H.A. Jennings died in 1937, he was succeeded by his son Erwin Strickland Jennings. H.A. Jennings had subtantial community involvement, evidenced by being a member of the Pequot Yacht club, and his achievement of 32nd degree 1ason at the Pyramid Temple of the Mystic Shrine. In 1941 the company was threatened by fire that caused $100,000 damge, overcame 13 firemen, and gutted the building, but they were able to resume business.

All Jennings Brothers pieces are marked somewhere with the letters JB. On the other hand, since the molds of the company were purchased by the Philadelphia Manufacturing Company (also known as PM Craftsman, or simply PMC) in the 1960s, recently manufactured examples of Jennings Brothers designs do exist. For instance, Plate 544 (New Bedford Whaler) has been seen as the original JB piece, as well as a recent reissue by PMC. Usually, the patina of the more recent pieces is easily discerned from the much earlier original JB creations. Sometimes the JB markings are not easily visible, but are instead placed in very out-of-the-way locations. JB pieces were made only of cast gray metal, but JB was also known for a silver-plating process they developed, so some silverplate pieces are likely to be seen. Their finishing processes made pieces of such quality that bronze finishes on cast gray metal pieces are easily mistaken for solid bronze. Indeed, there is no other major manufacturer with pieces whose finish remains as durable as that of JB, allowing one to often find pieces in pristine condition, though more than 50 years old. One catalog of JB pieces is reported to have more than 3,000 different offerings, to include such items as ashtrays, jewelry boxes, bookends, desk sets, figurines, paperweights, tea sets, candlesticks, table flatware, etc. At one time, the company had a showroom at the Gifts and Arts Center, 225 Fifth Avenue, New York.

Though obviously a drastic oversimplification, the basic process of metal casting went as follows: Once a mold of a figurine or statue was made, a bronze mold was then created, often in two pieces if simple, but perhaps with several separate pieces for legs or other parts as necessary. A spelter or similar type metal was poured into the bronze mold and when cold the mold was taken apart and a finish applied by a specially developed elecroplating process. The actual origin of a substantial portion of the subject matter is unknown: that is, none of the pieces are directly artist signed. On the other hand, many of the works are done by famous artists that are internationally recognized (e.g., the Lion of Lucerne; the Seated Lincoln by Daniel Chester; Pioneer Woman by Baker). Even so, we are uncertain as to how miniature versions of these famous pieces were obtained or constructed. Edward Austin Jennings is reported to have made jaunts to New York City to meet immigrants, Polish, Latvian, and Slavic peoples, whose entire families he successfully encouraged to become Jennings Brothers employees. At that time, Edward himself worked six days a week, and his factory workers (numbering about 125 during his leadership) worked five full days and half-day Saturday. Pieces were marketed at dog shows, horse shows, hunt clubs, and yachting events, as well as by various private stores. Business was at its peak in the 1920s and 1930s. During World War II, metal shortages redirected JB efforts away from their usual lines into production of hubcaps for military trucks. Post war imports of ceramic and plastic items drastically reduced demand and economic viability of the metal crafted items, leading to the eventual demise of the company. At the close of JB, molds were originally sold to a concrete block entrepreneur, who was unable to make an economic success of their use, but subsequently PMC has successfully obtained and used the orginal molds.

JUDD COMPANY

Morton Judd began a small machine shop and foundry in New Britain, Conn., in 1817, developed the M. Judd and Sons Company in 1830, and was eventually joined by all three of his sons in 1855. In the 1850s there was also a factory in New Haven, Conn. In 1870, H.L. Judd (one of Morton's sons) took over the company and the name was changed to H.L. Judd. Growth of the company resulted in a larger, more modern factory located in Brooklyn, New York, in 1875. Unfortunately, in 1884 a fire destroyed the factory. A new home was established in 1885 in Wallingford, Conn., as the permanent home of the new factory, administrative and sales offices remaining in New York City. H.L. Judd Company was acquired by Stanley Works in 1954, and became the Stanley-Judd Division, still located in Wallingford Conn.

Judd pieces are some of the highest quality iron pieces seen, with great attention to detail, enduring and interesting paint techniques, and durable two-piece construction in many cases. In addition to bookends, the company also made brass beds, ink wells, and fishing lures.

REFERENCES: Wallingford Public Library, local newspaper
Jubilee 300 – Wallingford Tercentenary, June 27 – July 4, 1970
Meriden-Wallingford B.I.E. Day (Business-Industry-Education) Book

LITTLESTOWN HARDWARE AND FOUNDRY CO. INC. (LITTCO)

Littco is still in operation at P.O. Box 69, Charles Street, Littlestown, Pennsylvania 17340 (717-359-4141). It was founded by Emory H. and Luther D. Snyder, two brothers who were engaged in 1915 in a hardware supply company. At that time they also operated a garage in Wrightsville (Pennsylvania). The Snyders moved to Littlestown, and in 1916 began a general hardware buying and selling business. Later that year an iron foundry developed and played a key role in the company's growth as a hardware manufacturer and supplier. The brothers remained active in the business until shortly before their deaths, one at age 97, the other at age 98.

In the 1920s and 30s, Littco brought out their bookends and doorstops. All pieces were manufactured in the Littlestown foundry, and marketing was handled by a sales agency at 225th Avenue, New York. Company executives report that designs for the bookends were sculpted by a local artist residing in Wrightsville. In 1941, the price of the most expensive bookend pair issued by Littco was 80 cents per pair (plus freight). World War II called up some of the employees, and raw materials were utilized for essentials only, so production of bookends and doorstops ceased. Of the more than 40 different kinds of bookends pictured in a Littco catalogue, all but one have been seen and identified, as well as numerous pieces that are not in the catalog. Littco pieces are generally very heavy, solid iron. Painted pieces are distinctly less common among bookends, but quite routine among doorstops.

MILLER BRASS FOUNDRY

The Miller Company is one of the oldest industrial plants in Meriden, beginning in 1844 as a producer of candlesticks and oil-burning lamps. In 1858, the process for distilling kerosene from bituminous coal was developed, and Miller was the first to design, produce, and market a kerosene-burning lamp. The company's progress paralleled the development in the lighting industry, as they initially made gas fixtures, then lamps using the Wellsbach mantle, then Edison's carbon filament incandescent lamp, the mercury-vapor lamp, and in 1938 fluorescent lamp.

In order to produce brass parts used in making lamps, Miller began a brass rolling mill in 1868, but soon expanded it to become a national supplier of phosphor bronze and brass. The Miller Company still exists today in Meriden. Only a single example of bookend work by Miller has been seen (Plate 241) which you will note is produced using the same design as the polychrome piece by K&O Company (Plate 240)

REFERENCE: *150 Years of Meriden*: Published in Connection with the Observance of the City's Sesquicentennial June 17-23, 1956.

NUART METAL CREATIONS

Nuart was apparently a subsidiary of The Gift House, Inc., which was located at 1107 Broadway in its 1931 catalog. In addition to bookends, the company made lamps, ashtrays, candlesticks, and paperweights. The 1931 catalog lists four different finishes for their products: bronze, ebony black, green, and oriental red.

The 1931 catalog lists 28 different pairs of bookends, but there were many more on the market. Nuart's most inventive pieces were Art Deco females, especially those designed for lamps. Unfortunately, the paint process was of a poorly enduring quality, and it is routine to find either flaked or unusually chipped off paint areas for pieces that have been, for the most part, well protected. Nuart used at least two shopmarks, one with the name spelled out in a linear fashion, the other with the name along the periphery of a circular imprint.

PAUL MORI AND SONS

Also known as Galavano Bronze, Paul Mori produced pieces in the bronze clad style, the earliest of which is pictured as Dante & Beatrice, and dated 1915. The company was located in New York City, and continued production through the 1920s.

REFERENCE: *Bookend Revue*, Seecof, Seecof and Kuritzky, Schiffer Publishers, 1996.

POMPEIAN BRONZE COMPANY

Little is known about the Pompeian Bronze Company. They have over 30 copyrights for bookends and other art metal goods, the first of which is dated 1921, the last 1930. During this period, their offices were at 603 Dean Street, Brooklyn, New York. No traditional cast bronze pieces are known by Pompeian Bronze, rather, they produced bronze clad, or heavy gray metal pieces. Often the bronze clad pieces are imprinted with the company name. Sometimes, the gray metal pieces merely have "PB, Inc.," but fortunately the gray metal pieces are often dated and named on the back. All copyrights are registered to Peter Maneredi, who may have been one of their designers.

RONSON

Ronson, variously labeled as LVA, LV Aronson, Louis V. Aronson, or Art Metal Works, is generally regarded as one of the most prolific, as well as most creative of all art metal bookend producers. The first art metal piece recorded in the U.S. copyright office is dated November 8, 1915, though we known that Mr. Aronson obtained a patent for one of his works in 1909. At the time of the initial 1915 work, the company was located at 9 Mulberry Street in Newark, New Jersey. Over 150 copyrights are registered to Aronson or Art Metal Works. It is usually not clear who is the artist/sculptor of the pieces. Many of those registered to Art Metal Works (1931 – 1937) are credited to Frederick Kaufmann, at the office location 46 Center St., Newark, NJ., and a few are credited to John Skiba.

A 1936 catalog of Art Metal Works, Inc. has more than one hundred and fifty examples of Ronson bookends. At that time, the central office of AMW is listed as Aronson Square, Newark, New Jersey, but letterhead details include permanent display rooms for AMW products in New York (347 Fifth Avenue), Chicago (136 South State Street), Los Angeles (728 South Flower Street), Canada (Dominion Art Metal Works, Toronto), England (Ronson Products, London), and Australia (W.G. Watson, & Co., Sydney). Ronson bookends were complemented with at least 16 different finishes, descriptions of some of which are:

Imperial Bronze: two-tone antique copper-bronze effect
Venetian Bronze: two-tone dull green-gold effect, hand relieved in verdi-green
Tyrrhian Bronze: two-tone dusty bronze effect with copper highlights
Royal Bronze: black-bronze effect, hand relieved in verdi-green
Polished Brass: traditional brass
Colonial Bronze: medium bronze effect combined with copper-colored highlights
Georgian Bronze: deep bronze effect combined with brass-colored highlights
Lincoln Bronze: two-toned green-gold effect, hand relieved in brown

Chromium Plate: high-gloss chrome finish
Copper: brilliant red-hued copper finish
Ebony: matte finish black
Decorated polished-gold effect: gold-colored metal with polychrome enameling
Depression green: creamy light green matte finish
Gun Metal: silver-gray glossy finish

SNEAD IRON WORKS

Snead Iron Works was founded in Louisville, Kentucky, in 1849. From that date until 1890 they fashioned ornament iron work. In 1890 they were awarded a contract from the government to replace the wood shelving in the Library of Congress, with metal. The company also produced shelving for the Vatican Library in Rome, the Sterling Library at Yale University, the National Archives Building in Washington, D. C., and other internationally known libraries. Countless individuals have tread the stairway in the Washington Monument, produced by Snead & Co. From 1897 until 1940, they were located in Jersey City, New Jersey, at which time they moved to Orange, Virginia.

Copyrights in the company name for bookends were issued as early as 1924 (the Madonna bookend, Plate 213, here, copyright #73078, December 1, 1924, by Olga Popoff Muller). All together, 10 copyrights are issued to this company for bookends, although they produced other art metal goods ("Wild Rose Candlesticks" copyright 1925, to Angus MacDonald of Snead and Company).

SYROCO, INC.

The Syracuse Ornamental Corporation currently is housed at 7528 State Fair Boulevard, Baldwinsville, New York 13027 (31 635-9911 Ext. 2242).The company had its origins in 1890. A group of European craftsmen soon were in great demand as a resu of the hand-carved fashion pieces they provided for fine homes and institutions, including the Governor's Mansion in Albany. In a effort to make such styles available on a wider scale, a technique was developed of molding reproductions by compressing a mi ture of waxes, woodflour, and resin. This type of product was used primarily to provide carving details to furniture. After World W II, Syroco developed a line of home decorative accessories, including many bookends. Syroco bookends most often have a suppo plate attached to the resin figure, with natural wood hue the most common finish, although pieces are also available in a variety colors. The company's historical records were lost in a recent fire, preventing greater insight into the company's history.

METALS

The majority of bookends of primary interest to collectors are metal. Although sophisticated scientific techniques (e.g spectophotometry) can identify metals with exacting precision, accurate identification by means of simple judgments an hands-on techniques are adequate for the purposes of most enthusiasts. Bookends are generally not composed of preciou metals, hence the composition metal is often not the determining factor of its value or interest. Unless you know the sourc from which you are purchasing bookends is knowledgeable about metal composition, you must determine to your own satis faction the makeup of the materials. Often, pieces are specifically designed to mimic the appearance of bronze or brass, n with the intent to deceive the purchaser, but rather to improve the artistic appeal of the piece. It is easy to mistake iron, ca gray metal, or other metals for bronze.

It is not always possible to determine with certainty the composition of nonferrous metals without specialized testin Every interested person should carry a simple refrigerator magnet or similar piece that can be applied to metal surfaces t see if they are ferrous (i.e., contain iron). Iron will always attract the magnet, even if well coated with other materials. plastic, thick paint, or even a coating of another metal or some sort of plating process has been used to decorate the exter or of the piece, the magnetic field created by iron will attract the magnet.

Any metal which attracts the magnet must be iron, though you may hear protestations from dealers who have unfort nately purchased the piece themselves believing it to be bronze or brass on the basis of appearance. Also, there are piece which look very much like iron which are bronze, brass, or some other metal.

For instance, I was confident that Riderless Horse, Plate 487 in this book, was composed of iron, having seen many exam ples with a variety of paint finishes, rusted iron, etc. As I was demonstrating to an interested friend the necessity of applying magnet to every piece, voilá!...no stick: it was bronze! The fact that each of the many examples I had seen previously had bee made of iron led to my anticipation that this one was also. In discussions with relatives of individuals who owned or worked i foundries, I have learned it was fairly commonplace for foundries to "borrow" popular pieces from other companies and recas them in their own style, materials, finishes, and detail. In general, bronze pieces exhibit the greatest degree of detail, but c course this is not always the case. You will see side-by-side comparisons of identical pieces cast in bronze, brass, iron, c other metals, and note how usually it is quite easy to differentiate the detail of a bronze casting from iron. In general, bronz or brass is a more prized composition than are other metals, though there are collectors who specifically prefer one of th other metals. Additionally, pieces made of cast gray metal are no less desirable to collectors; many of the pieces most soug after by collectors (e.g., Ronson, Jennings Brothers, Frankart, K&O Company) were cast exclusively in gray metal.

Bookends can be composed of different metals in different parts. Be sure to test each separate portion individually because sometimes the base will be composed of iron, but the figure will be of another metal.

Metals can be differentiated on the basis of their temperature to the touch. It will take some practice to learn this, but if you sit down for a moment and compare, for instance, iron, brass, bronze, cast gray metal, you will find that brass is the coldest, iron next cold, bronze next, and gray metal is about room temperature, or very slightly cool.

Another method of metal identification requires scratching the surface with a hard, sharp tool. Since this method leaves a scratch on the metal surface, it should only be done on the underside, or some other inconspicuous place and of course, with the permission of the person who owns the piece. Some antique purveyors are very hesitant to allow you to lift the felt piece off the bottom of the bookend to test it, but others do not mind in the least, and are quite interested to learn the composition themselves.

CASTING METHODS

Charcoal casting is an ancient technique which, though imprecise, is simple and efficient. Molten metal is poured or pressed into a mold carved from charcoal.

Sand casting is performed by pressing moist sand tightly around a model which is then removed. The resulting mold cavity is filled with molten metal. Although any sand can work, specially prepared casting sand is preferred. Sand is prepared by mixing with water or oil until it holds together when squeezed into a ball.

Lost wax process casting has been used since antiquity. Initially, models were made from beeswax and then coated with layers of clay. After the outer layers had been sufficiently reinforced, with straw or linen, the clay-over-beeswax model was oven-hardened. In this process, the wax burned away, leaving behind a solid reinforced clay vessel, into whose cavity molten metal could be poured. After pouring the metal and hardening, the outer clay shell is broken and discarded. This method is also known as the waste mold casting method, after the destruction of the mold in the process.

REFERENCE: *The Complete Metalsmith*, Tim McCreight, Davis Publication, Worcester, Massachusetts, 1991.

ALUMINUM

Aluminum is uncommonly used to produce bookends, but several examples have been seen. In 1884 when the Washington Monument was completed, a 100 ounce pyramid of aluminum was placed at the top, reported to be the largest aluminum mass ever produced up until that time. In New York City, the piece was actually displayed in Tiffany's window prior to being installed in the monument. Aluminum is desirable in industry because of its light weight, resistance to corrosion, and ability to combine well with other metals. An international system is devised to identify other metals with which aluminum is alloyed, designated as the first digit of a four digit number (other digits refer to other properties):

1xxx = essentially pure aluminum
2xxx = copper alloy
3xxx = manganese alloy
4xxx = silicon alloy
5xxx = magnesium alloy
6xxx = magnesium and silicon alloy
7xxx = zinc alloy
8xxx = other elements

BRASS

Brass dates back to the Neolithic Age, possibly a result of accidental reduction of zinc and copper ores. Some experts suggest that brass and bronze are used interchangeably when referring to ancient metals. Brass is an alloy of copper and zinc, resulting in a product that is malleable, machinable, and resistant to corrosion, as well as being more hardy than either of its constituents.

The dominant component of brass is copper (about 70%). The greater the percentage copper, the greater the malleability and intensity of color, which is maximum at about 90% copper (red brass). Alpha brasses are used for such things as screws, pins, and bolts, and are known for malleability and cold working properties. Brass used for fashion jewelry (e.g., Pinchbeck, NuGold) is often in the 88/12 alloy range.

BRONZE

Bronze was used as early as 3000 B.C. and is an alloy of copper and tin. Bronze is more easily melted and cast than copper, and less susceptible to corrosion. Bell metal, which received its name because of the type of tone it produces when struck, typically has 14-25% tin. Statuary bronze may have as little as 10% tin. Zinc or phosphorus is sometimes added to bronze to improve strength and quality. To tell the difference between brass and bronze, use of a 50/50 solution of nitric acid and water produces a white precipitate (metastannic acid) in the presence of tin. Distinguishing between bronze and brass is most often of academic interest only.

CHROMIUM

Employed on a number of pieces pictured in this volume, chromium was discovered in 1789 by a French chemis. Chromium is noteworthy for its ability to form alloys, hardness, and sheen. Since it is heat and corrosion resistant, it is useful coating, but pieces are generally not molded out of chromium alone because it is too difficult to stamp, form, a mold bulk chromium. Nonetheless, chromium may not be well suited as a covering for metals that are highly rust-susceptib such as iron, since microscopic holes in the chromium allow moisture penetration which will eventually result in peeling excoriation of the chromium covering. For this reason, metals that are highly corrosion (e.g., brass and bronze) are excelle base substances for chromium plating, as the surface will never tarnish, peel off, or require polishing. Chase Brass & Co per Company capitalized on these desirable aspects of chromium for many of their popular products.

REFERENCE: *Art Deco Chrome* Book 2, Richard Kilbride, Jo-D Books, Stamford, CT, 1992.

COPPER

More than 100 alloys of copper are available. Metal craftsmen generally prefer a process called cold-rolling whic leaves a smooth surface, as opposed to hot-rolling, which leaves a rough surface.

Oxidation of copper in air forms a variety of oxides (acetates, sulfates, chlorides) which are called verdigris, from t Old French "vert-de-grice," or "green of Greece," harkening back to metal sculpture typical of ancient Grecian sculptors.

These oxides are toxic to copper workers who must pay rigorous attention to hand washing to avoid toxicity. Deoxidizers li phosphorous are often alloyed with copper to avoid copper oxide production, which tends to substantially weaken the metal.

IRON AND STEEL

Sulfur, phosphorous, silicon, and carbon are common constituents of iron ore. The smelting process results in 3-4% ca bon, and produces a metal, capable of being poured, called cast iron or pig iron. The American Iron and Steel Industry (AIS used this code system: B 1065

type of furnace used in smelting (B for Bessemer)
first 2 digits, major alloying material (10 for carbon)
last 2 digits, % in this alloy (0.65% carbon)

Steel is commonly alloyed. Chromium helps to resist corrosion; stainless steel is 10-20% chromium. Manganese increases har ness; molybdenum increases corrosion resistance, and tungsten produces tungsten carbide particles that are abrasion resistant.

The primary difference between steel and cast iron is the relative plasticity of steel. Cast iron is a complex alloy, pr dominately iron, carbon, and silicon; silicon is very influential in the properties of the metal. Carbon content of cast ir (2.54%) is substantially higher than that of most steel. Manganese, sulfur, and phosphorus are also present in all cast iro but sometimes copper, molybdenum, nickel, and chromium are added. Cast irons are grouped into one of three main cat gories: gray, white, and malleable. The gray and white refer to the appearance of ruptured ends of the metal. Malleable ca iron, of course, refers to its ability to undergo some formation without fracture.

NICKEL

The word "nickel" comes from the German word meaning "deceiver," in reference to its being easily mistaken for copp ore. Alloying metals with nickel increases hardness and resistance to corrosion. The most common alloy used in metal cra ing is nickel silver, also known as German silver or white brass, composed of 60% copper, 20% nickel and 20% zinc. Nick is a very common contact allergen which can cause quite a problem since it is frequently used in earrings, necklaces, sci sors, door handles, watchbands, bracelets, and belt buckles, resulting in an unpleasant rash in persons who are sensitive it. To help people allergic to nickel, a testing kit based upon dimethylgloyoxime is available, enabling them to identify th presence of nickel in jewelry, etc. If a pink color is produced, nickel is present.

SILVER

Because pure silver is too soft to be practical when used alone, it is alloyed, most often with copper. Addition of copp allows increasing strength, without reduction of the shine which makes silver so desirable.

King Henry II of England in the twelfth century imported a silver alloy which was adopted as the standard, and is mo often used in jewelry and silversmithing. This alloy was from Easterling Germany, and by 1300 it came to be used for curre cy and known as "Sterling" silver.

Coin silver contains 10-20% copper, but is subject to tarnish. A 90% alloy was used in United States coins until 1966.

Cleaning of silver can be done with hand polishing, but recently electrolytic cleaning has become popular. The process done by using an aluminum-surfaced container with a solution of equal parts baking soda, salt, and liquid soap, typically cup each per gallon of water. When tarnished silver is placed into the heated mixture for just a few minutes, oxides are tran ferred to the aluminum; after this process, simple soap and water rinse is sufficient.

WHITE METALS
(Also called gray metals)

This is a general term, used to designate a variety of soft metals with low melting points. The most consistent ingredients are lead, tin, cadmium, and bismuth. Although any of the individual components has a very high melting point (greater than 450 degrees Fahrenheit), alloying them in various proportions reduces the melting point to less than 200 degrees, allowing the multi-ingredient alloy to be readily melted and cast. Commonly known as pot metal, or type metal, because of its use in making printers' type, these metals are moderately corrosion resistant, but because of their low melting point are difficult to repair. Sometimes white metals are mistakenly called spelter which is a term for zinc. When brass is used as a solder for steel in the process of brazing, it is also called spelter.

PEWTER AND BRITANNIA

The alloy used in colonial America was a lead/tin combination. Later in the 1700s in England, another alloy was developed (91% tin, 7% antimony, 2% copper), called Britannia Metal, and today the terms are often considered interchangeable.

SPELTER

Spelter is zinc, refined to 99.97%. Sometimes this is confused with cast gray metal, or pot metal, but they are distinctly different. Spelter has been used to produce high quality figures sometimes called French Bronze, since the subject matter or molds are often French in origin, the figures are produced to standards of bronze (the same weight and thickness), and the spelter shares some characteristics of bronze. For instance, pot metal (cast gray metal) cannot be "healed"; damaged parts cannot be fused without melting and distorting neighboring metal. On the other hand, spelter can be joined by brazing, and hence complex designs using multi-section methods can be used for production, and the metal can be repaired, as can bronze. Favorable qualities of spelter include its resistance to deterioration with time and atmospheric conditions.

Reference: *The Complete Metalsmith*, Tim McCreight, Davis Publications, Worcester, Massachusetts, 1991.

Metallurgy, Carl G. Johnson, William R. Weeks, American Technical Society, Chicago, Illinois, 1956.

PLASTICS

Synthetic materials that are processed by heat molding and formed to a final shape are called plastic. There are more than 40 basic plastic families with distinctly different characteristics. There are two major categories of plastics: thermoplastic and thermoset plastics.

The remarkable feature of thermoplastic is that it requires heat to make it formable, and once cooled, can be reheated and reformed into a new shape numerous times without a significant change in chemical properties. Similar to simple paraffin wax, thermoplastic material can be repeatedly melted by heat and solidified by cooling. Polyethylene, polystyrene, PVC, cellulosics, ABS, and nylon are examples of thermoplastics.

Thermoset plastic is heated to make its shape permanent, but cannot be remelted or reformed. Phenolics, as used in the Fleuron Company product Durez, and melamine, as used in dinnerware, are both examples of thermoset plastic.

BAKELITE

Bakelite was developed for use in industrial applications, molded automotive, and electrical parts. It was the first fully synthetic thermoset plastic, developed by Leo Henrick Baekeland, of Yonkers, New York. Baekeland actually discovered Bakelite while seeking to develop a varnish. Although he found that his resinous materials from formaldehyde and phenol so strongly resisted solvents and melting that they were worthless as a source of varnish, nonetheless these same characteristics were ideal for use in electrical and industrial projects. He announced his discovery at the Chemists Club of New York City, February 6, 1909. Colorful forms of the resin plastic weren't produced until the Depression. Bakelite Cast Resinoid was a clear liquid that could be colored, and cast or poured into molds and baked.

The American Catalin Corporation (New York, established 1927) was the foremost producer of Catalin, cast phenolic resin, for jewelry. By 1935 Modern Plastics magazine reported that 70% of women sported jewelry made from cast phenolics. By the 1950s the wave of enthusiasm had subsided, but an enthusiastic revival of interest in Bakelite products of all types is prevalent today.

CELLULOID

The origins of celluloid as a substitute for ivory began in the 1860s, with the commentary of Michael Phelan, an English billiards expert. At the time, ivory from Ceylon was felt to be the best substance for billiard balls, but was becoming increasingly expensive. In 1863, the American company Phelan and Collander stimulated progress away from the use of ivory by instituting a $10,000 prize to the first inventor who could develop a satisfactory substance for use in billiard balls.

PLASTICS

John Wesley Hyatt, a printer from Albany, New York, developed a composition product of paper pulp and gum shellac and used it to create checkers and dominoes. His company was called The Embossing Company. Even though these composition materials were effective as checkers, dominoes, and other toys, they were not enough like ivory to use as billiard balls. An accidental discovery did eventually lead to success.

At the time, printers used Collodion, a solution of pyroxylin, composed of nitrocellulose and alcohol, as a protective film on their hands, since it dried into a waterproof, elastic film. One day a dried-up spill of Collodion attracted the attention of Hyatt, who thought its hard, pliable, dense characteristics might be appropriate for billiard balls. His next step was to make a coating of this Collodion to apply to his composition billiard ball.

This combination had some substantial limitations: the nitrocellulose-based coating was highly flammable, and indeed more than once, exposure to a cigar flame had caused the balls to ignite. A Colorado saloon proprietor reported the somewhat unsettling experience when Collodion-coated billiard balls would collide with a resounding bang like that of a percussion gun cap, and patrons drew their guns! Even though these billiard balls tended to attract dirt, were difficult to clean, and were subject to burst into flames with modest provocation, these deterrents did not outweigh their inexpensiveness, and billiards began to expand from a pastime of the wealthy to the general population.

In 1869 John and his brother Isaiah modified the coating by adding camphor as a solvent and using heat and pressure application. The new product was named Celluloid, either a combination of colloid and cellulose, or simply a word meaning "cellulose-like." This product was the first semi-synthetic thermoplastic. Eventually, the methodology evolved into using solid Celluloid for billiard balls, and these were free of the problems of flammability, noise, and appearance that had plagued previous products.

By the 1890s, Celluloid manufacture had been refined to the point that the product was used effectively to substitute for amber, coral, ivory, jet, and tortoise. Numerous American and foreign companies developed additional similar products with such names as Pyralin, Fiberloid, and Viscoloid, but most are grouped generically under the term celluloid. There are divergent reports about whether or not Mr. Hyatt ever received his prize money for developing Celluloid.

Twentieth century Celluloid is generally composed of cellulose fiber, camphor, nitric acid, sulfuric acid, and ethyl alcohol. Twentieth century manufacturers include Arling Company (owned by DuPont), Fiberloid (later Monsanto), Viscoloid (Leominster, Massachusetts), and Celluloid Corporation, Newark, New Jersey. In the 1920s a nonflammable formulation obtained by substituting acetic acid for nitrocellulose, called Lumarith, replaced many previous Celluloid uses. Celluloid production in the U.S. ceased in the late 1940s, by which time the Celluloid Company had become part of Celanese Corporation and further refinements of plastics replaced Celluloid.

Cleaning of Celluloid can be done with mild soap, warm water, and a soft brush or cloth. Vegetable oil, left in place for a few minutes and rubbed off with a soft cloth, is also reported to be effective. Nail polish remover, detergents, window cleaner solution, and the like may react chemically with Celluloid and damage it.

REFERENCE: Robinson, Julie, *Antique Week*, Volume 28, Number 13, June 19, 1995.

INDEX

INDEX

COLLECTOR BOOKS

Informing Today's Collector

*For over two decades we have been keeping collectors informed
on trends and values in all fields of antiques and collectibles.*

BOOKS ON GLASS AND POTTERY

1810	American Art Glass, Shuman	$29.95
1312	Blue & White Stoneware, McNerney	$9.95
1959	Blue Willow, 2nd Ed., Gaston	$14.95
4553	Coll. Glassware from the 40's, 50's, 60's, 3rd Ed., Florence	$19.95
3816	Collectible Vernon Kilns, Nelson	$24.95
3311	Collecting Yellow Ware – Id. & Value Gd., McAllister	$16.95
1373	Collector's Ency. of American Dinnerware, Cunningham	$24.95
3815	Coll. Ency. of Blue Ridge Dinnerware, Newbound	$19.95
2272	Collector's Ency. of California Pottery, Chipman	$24.95
3811	Collector's Ency. of Colorado Pottery, Carlton	$24.95
3312	Collector's Ency. of Children's Dishes, Whitmyer	$19.95
2133	Collector's Ency. of Cookie Jars, Roerig	$24.95
3723	Coll. Ency. of Cookie Jars-Volume II, Roerig	$24.95
4552	Collector's Ency. of Depression Glass, 12th Ed., Florence	$19.95
2209	Collector's Ency. of Fiesta, 7th Ed., Huxford	$19.95
1439	Collector's Ency. of Flow Blue China, Gaston	$19.95
3812	Coll. Ency. of Flow Blue China, 2nd Ed., Gaston	$24.95
3813	Collector's Ency. of Hall China, 2nd Ed., Whitmyer	$24.95
2334	Collector's Ency. of Majolica Pottery, Katz-Marks	$19.95
1358	Collector's Ency. of McCoy Pottery, Huxford	$19.95
3313	Collector's Ency. of Niloak, Gifford	$19.95
3837	Collector's Ency. of Nippon Porcelain I, Van Patten	$24.95
2089	Collector's Ency. of Nippon Porcelain II, Van Patten	$24.95
1665	Collector's Ency. of Nippon Porcelain III, Van Patten	$24.95
4712	Collector's Ency. of Nippon Porcelain IV, Van Patten	$24.95
1447	Collector's Ency. of Noritake, 1st Series, Van Patten	$19.95
1034	Collector's Ency. of Roseville Pottery, Huxford	$19.95
1035	Collector's Ency. of Roseville Pottery, 2nd Ed., Huxford	$19.95
3314	Collector's Ency. of Van Briggle Art Pottery, Sasicki	$24.95
2339	Collector's Guide to Shawnee Pottery, Vanderbilt	$19.95
1425	Cookie Jars, Westfall	$9.95
3440	Cookie Jars, Book II, Westfall	$19.95
2275	Czechoslovakian Glass & Collectibles, Barta	$16.95
4716	Elegant Glassware of the Depression Era, 7th Ed., Florence	$19.95
3725	Fostoria - Pressed, Blown & Hand Molded Shapes, Kerr	$24.95
3883	Fostoria Stemware - The Crystal for America, Long	$24.95
3886	Kitchen Glassware of the Depression Years, 5th Ed., Florence	$19.95
4772	McCoy Pottery, Coll. Reference & Value Guide, Hanson	$19.95
4725	Pocket Guide to Depression Glass, 10th Ed., Florence	$9.95
3825	Puritan Pottery, Morris	$24.95
1670	Red Wing Collectibles, DePasquale	$9.95
1440	Red Wing Stoneware, DePasquale	$9.95
1958	So. Potteries Blue Ridge Dinnerware, 3rd Ed., Newbound	$14.95
4634	Standard Carnival Glass, 5th Ed., Edwards	$24.95
3327	Watt Pottery – Identification & Value Guide, Morris	$19.95
2224	World of Salt Shakers, 2nd Ed., Lechner	$24.95

BOOKS ON DOLLS & TOYS

4707	A Decade of Barbie Dolls and Collectibles, 1981 - 1991, Summers	$19.95
2079	Barbie Fashion, Vol. 1, 1959-1967, Eames	$24.95
3310	Black Dolls – 1820 - 1991 – Id. & Value Guide, Perkins	$17.95
1529	Collector's Ency. of Barbie Dolls, DeWein	$19.95
2338	Collector's Ency. of Disneyana, Longest & Stern	$24.95
3727	Coll. Guide to Ideal Dolls, Izen	$18.95

4645	Madame Alexander Price Guide #21, Smith	$9.95
4723	Matchbox Toys, 1947 to 1996, Johnson	$18.95
4647	Modern Collector's Dolls, 8th series, Smith	$24.95
1540	Modern Toys, 1930 - 1980, Baker	$19.95
4640	Patricia Smith's Doll Values – Antique to Modern, 12th ed.	$12.95
4728	Schroeder's Coll. Toys, 3rd Edition	$17.95
3826	Story of Barbie, Westenhouser, No Values	$19.95
2028	Toys, Antique & Collectible, Longest	$14.95
1808	Wonder of Barbie, Manos	$9.95
1430	World of Barbie Dolls, Manos	$9.95

OTHER COLLECTIBLES

1457	American Oak Furniture, McNerney	$9.95
3716	American Oak Furniture, Book II, McNerney	$12.95
4704	Antique & Collectible Buttons, Wisniewski	$19.95
2333	Antique & Collectible Marbles, 3rd Ed., Grist	$9.95
1748	Antique Purses, Holiner	$19.95
1426	Arrowheads & Projectile Points, Hothem	$7.95
1278	Art Nouveau & Art Deco Jewelry, Baker	$9.95
1714	Black Collectibles, Gibbs	$19.95
4708	B.J. Summers' Guide to Coca-Cola, Summers	$19.95
1128	Bottle Pricing Guide, 3rd Ed., Cleveland	$7.95
3717	Christmas Collectibles, 2nd Ed., Whitmyer	$24.95
1752	Christmas Ornaments, Johnson	$19.95
3718	Collectible Aluminum, Grist	$16.95
2132	Collector's Ency. of American Furniture, Vol. I, Swedberg	$24.95
2271	Collector's Ency. of American Furniture, Vol. II, Swedberg	$24.95
3720	Coll. Ency. of American Furniture, Vol III, Swedberg	$24.95
3722	Coll. Ency. of Compacts, Carryalls & Face Powder Boxes, Mueller	$24.95
2018	Collector's Ency. of Granite Ware, Greguire	$24.95
3430	Coll. Ency. of Granite Ware, Book 2, Greguire	$24.95
1441	Collector's Guide to Post Cards, Wood	$9.95
2276	Decoys, Kangas	$24.95
1716	Fifty Years of Fashion Jewelry, Baker	$19.95
4568	Flea Market Trader, 10th Ed., Huxford	$12.95
3819	General Store Collectibles, Wilson	$24.95
3436	Grist's Big Book of Marbles, Everett Grist	$19.95
2278	Grist's Machine Made & Contemporary Marbles	$9.95
1424	Hatpins & Hatpin Holders, Baker	$9.95
4721	Huxford's Collectible Advertising – Id. & Value Gd., 3rd Ed	$24.95
4648	Huxford's Old Book Value Guide, 8th Ed.	$19.95
1181	100 Years of Collectible Jewelry, Baker	$9.95
2216	Kitchen Antiques – 1790 - 1940, McNerney	$14.95
4724	Modern Guns – Id. & Val. Gd., 11th Ed., Quertermous	$12.95
2026	Railroad Collectibles, 4th Ed., Baker	$14.95
1632	Salt & Pepper Shakers, Guarnaccia	$9.95
1888	Salt & Pepper Shakers II, Guarnaccia	$14.95
2220	Salt & Pepper Shakers III, Guarnaccia	$14.95
3443	Salt & Pepper Shakers IV, Guarnaccia	$18.95
4727	Schroeder's Antiques Price Guide, 15th Ed.	$14.95
4729	Sewing Tools & Trinkets, Thompson	$24.95
2096	Silverplated Flatware, 4th Ed., Hagan	$14.95
2348	20th Century Fashionable Plastic Jewelry, Baker	$19.95
3828	Value Guide to Advertising Memorabilia, Summers	$18.95
3830	Vintage Vanity Bags & Purses, Gerson	$24.95

This is only a partial listing of the books on antiques that are available from Collector Books. All books are well illustrated and contain current values. Most of these books are available from your local book seller, antique dealer, or public library. If you are unable to locate certain titles in your area, you may order by mail from COLLECTOR BOOKS, P.O. Box 3009, Paducah, KY 42002-3009. Customers with Visa or MasterCard may phone in orders from 7:00–5:00 CST, Monday–Friday, Toll Free 1-800-626-5420. Add $2.00 for postage for the first book ordered and $0.30 for each additional book. Include item number, title, and price when ordering. Allow 14 to 21 days for delivery.

Schroeder's ANTIQUES Price Guide

. . . is the #1 best-selling antiques & collectibles value guide on the market today, and here's why . . .

Schroeder's ANTIQUES Price Guide

OUR #1 BEST SELLER!

Identification & Values Of Over 50,000 Antiques & Collectibles

8½ x 11, 608 Pages, $12.95

- *More than 300 advisors, well-known dealers, and top-notch collectors work together with our editors to bring you accurate information regarding pricing and identification.*

- *More than 45,000 items in almost 500 categories are listed along with hundreds of sharp original photos that illustrate not only the rare and unusual, but the common, popular collectibles as well.*

- *Each large close-up shot shows important details clearly. Every subject is represented with histories and background information, a feature not found in any of our competitors' publications.*

- *Our editors keep abreast of newly developing trends, often adding several new categories a year as the need arises.*

If it merits the interest of today's collector, you'll find it in *Schroeder's*. And you can feel confident that the information we publish is up to date and accurate. Our advisors thoroughly check each category to spot inconsistencies, listings that may not be entirely reflective of market dealings, and lines too vague to be of merit. Only the best of the lot remains for publication.

Without doubt, you'll find
SCHROEDER'S ANTIQUES PRICE GUIDE
the only one to buy for
reliable information and values.

COLLECTOR BOOKS
A Division of Schroeder Publishing Co., Inc.